MODERN
OUTDOOR
SURVIVAL

MODERN OUTDOOR SURVIVAL

Outdoor Gear and Savvy
to Bring You Back Alive

Dwight R. Schuh

MENASHA RIDGE PRESS
Birmingham, Alabama

Copyright © 1979, 1983 by Dwight R. Schuh
First Menasha Edition, First printing, 1989

Published by Menasha Ridge Press
P. O. Box 59257, Birmingham, Alabama 35259-9257

Library of Congress Cataloging-in-Publication Data

Schuh, Dwight R.
    Modern outdoor survival.

    Reprint. Originally published: New York : Arco, 1983.
    Includes index.
    1. Wilderness survival.   2. Outdoor life — Equipment and
supplies.   I. Title.
[GV200.5.S38 1989]   613.6'9   88-8342
ISBN 0-89732-054-9

Printed in the United States of America

This book is dedicated to our daughter,
Emily Ruth,
two weeks old as I finish this book.

ACKNOWLEDGMENTS

For generously sharing their outdoors experience I want to thank Ed Beverly, Steve Byman, Billie Chambers, Ken Comfort, J. S. Hayward, Ph.D., Scott Heywood, Lee Juillerat, Doug Kittredge, Ed Little, Dennis Loomis, Bob Newman, Ed Park, Tom Poore, Jim Rawles, David Richey, Dr. Findlay Russell, Doug Shorey, Don Stonehill, Dick Suber, Bruce Wadlington, and Dave Williams.

I owe special thanks to Alden Glidden, M.D., Everett Howard, M.D., and Ken Magee, M.D. for their contributions in time and research materials.

And I owe special thanks to my mother, Josephine Schuh, for her typing efforts, and to my wife, Laura, for her typing, proofreading, and general patience and support.

CONTENTS

1
MODERN SURVIVAL

The idea of survival seems to inspire images of a bedraggled individual eating wild roots or berries, snaring squirrels and rabbits, locating hidden springs for water, building a fire by rubbing sticks together. Survival training seems to imply a need to survive for months in the wilds of northern Canada or the Sahara Desert, struggling against the elements with no hope of aid from the outside world. Survival seems to demand knowing how to live off the land.

Is this really modern survival? The fact is, most of us will never be in a position where primitive skills for living off the land are necessary. The world of modern recreation just doesn't make such demands. Within the continental United States, wilderness areas are criss-crossed with trails, and these areas have shrunk so that even in the most remote places, such as the Bob Marshall Wilderness in Montana or the River of No Return Wilderness, a person is never more than a couple of days from civilization.

Modern transportation and communication have further diminished the magnitude of wilderness. Prolonged isolation is almost impossible. The lost or stranded person often can be sighted within minutes by observers in airplanes. Helicopters can evacuate the injured quickly. Four-wheel-drive rigs can penetrate many remote regions in summer, and snowmobiles can do the same in winter. Two-way radio systems broadcast our plight and coordinate search-and-rescue efforts. Emergency rescue units form a network of instant aid.

Advanced equipment and knowledge also contribute to modern survival. The day of the blanket roll, packboard, fresh food, and open fire is past. Lightweight packframes, synthetic sleeping bags, folding water jugs, miniature stoves, canned heat, flyweight tents, boots for every situation, plastic canoes and aluminum boats, freeze-dried foods, and other modern equipment take most of the burden out of recreation. In addition, today we understand the physiology of hypothermia, heatstroke, and shock. We know how to prevent infection. We know how to treat snakebite and other injuries and illness. The point is that today we're blessed with equipment and knowledge equal to any survival situation or emergency. Little excuse exists for going into the field ill-prepared. In this age, a person has to be grossly careless or irresponsible to find himself in a predicament that demands primitive skills for survival.

I don't mean to play down the importance of survival knowledge. Despite modern innovations and knowledge, the outdoors has many potential dangers. Two common ones are hypothermia and heatstroke. Drowning takes many lives every year. People get lost, and they suffer injuries. Nature threatens with blizzards, lightning, and avalanches. Bear attacks are fairly frequent. So is snakebite. These and other survival threats face modern outdoorsmen just as they did the mountain men of a century ago, so survival knowledge is as important today as it was then. The level of that knowledge simply has changed.

Determining what constitutes modern survival knowledge will first of all demand a definition of a "survival situation." If a survival situation isn't a predicament in which we must know how to live off the land, then what is it?

The dictionary says that to survive means to "remain alive and existent." Survival, then, is the state of remaining alive.

Does anyone ever go into the outdoors without the desire to stay alive? Of course not. We all plan to live through every outdoor activity. So survival situations include much more than just outdoors emergencies and life-threatening predicaments. All outings, right down to the routine family picnic, are survival situations, and survival knowledge is any knowledge needed to make these outings safe. Survival is largely a matter of prevention, with emphasis on safety, caution, foresight, and preparation. But since even the most cautious and well-prepared person may still be hit by an emergency, treatment and rescue measures are also important elements of survival knowledge.

We all hope to live through every outdoor activity, but emergencies arise and test how well we're prepared to cope with the unexpected.

In our knowledge of a specialized subject, principles can often be more useful than rules. Memorized rules may be forgotten when needed most. Principles, by contrast, can lead to responsible action even when specifics aren't known. A foundation of principles is what we often call common sense, probably the most valuable asset in outdoors survival. Let's take a close look at some important principles in outdoor survival:

• **Outdoors emergencies are rarely acts of God.** Few people perish because of circumstances beyond their control. People usually perish because of their own lack of control. Nobody can govern the elements, but everyone can control his or her own actions. These actions, not conditions, generally determine whether a person survives.

• **Disaster can happen to you.** No one is immune. Dennis Loomis, a member of the Sheridan, Wyoming search-and-rescue (SAR) unit, says people's failure to recognize and admit this possibility precipitates many emergencies.

"Even after we spent two days to find one guy," Loomis says, "he wouldn't admit he was lost. He knew where he was. Just nobody else did.

"That's a dangerous attitude," Loomis goes on. "Anybody can get hurt. Anybody can lose his bearings in a fog. One big reason people get into trouble is that they go into the woods with the old idea that 'It can't happen to me.'"

• **Emergencies can happen at any time.** You don't have to be on a backcountry expedition to get into trouble. Bruce Wadlington of Crater Lake National Park in Oregon says one unsuspecting family, driving the main park road, stopped for a walk. They'd gone only 200 yards when they got separated in the fog. The father, dressed in shorts and tennis shoes, couldn't find the others and got lost. Park employees eventually found him jogging down a road 14 miles away. Only his being in good condition saved him from exposure in the 45° F.

weather. This near-disaster began with a 200-yard walk. Disaster can strike anywhere and anytime.

• **You should plan for the worst.** Complacency is dangerous. Search-and-rescue personnel I've talked to say that few people carry emergency gear or even have a map and compass. Few know the first-aid basics that could save a life.

Going outdoors is a lot like driving a car. Racing professionals always wear seat belts, not because they plan to crash but because the possibility always exists and they want to live through it if it happens. A person should approach outdoors activities the same way. Even if the sky is clear, prepare for snow; if your health is perfect, prepare for illness; if you've never seen a rattlesnake, prepare for a snakebite. Hope for the best and plan for the worst. You'll never be caught off-guard.

• **Prevention is the best medicine.** Avoiding emergencies is always easier and less painful than coping with them. That's why this book stresses safety, preparation, and caution.

• **Learn to live with the outdoors, not to fight it.** In this age of comfort, we feel threatened in any unusual situations. When we're caught outdoors with no tent or sleeping bag, we feel exposed and defenseless. When we lose our bearings, we feel lost. When we're injured in the backcountry, disaster seems imminent. When food runs out in the field, we seem to be starving. Overcoming these feelings is a big step toward outdoors survival. Panic under stressful conditions only breeds foolish actions.

Experienced woodsmen put emergencies into perspective. They know darkness is no threat, that with calm thought they'll find their way, that their first-aid knowledge is sufficient to handle injuries, that they're not going to starve to death. They don't fight circumstances. They know a cool head is their key to survival.

Modern Survival is for the average outdoorsman. It deals primarily with activities traditionally considered purely outdoors—hunting, hiking, fishing, camping, canoeing, backpacking, cross-country skiing, snowshoeing, and snowmobiling. But the same principles apply to all related recreation such as downhill skiing, sailing, and bicycling. However, mountain climbing, major expeditions, and certain other specialized forms of recreation require knowledge and training beyond the scope of this book.

Simply reading *Modern Survival* or any other book won't make you a survival expert. You can read how to use a map and compass, how to make a desert still, or how to build a lean-to shelter, and reading is a good start. But until you've done these things, you're a novice. Don't put off the gaining of such experience. When you're hungry, tired, cold, and confused is no time to get your first emergency survival experience. Now is the time to practice and learn; now is the time to assemble the needed equipment. If you take the time to prepare now, you'll be ready when your survival is at stake.

This book, of course, can't give you common sense, force you to prepare ahead of time, or make you cautious or observant. It can only offer guidelines and principles— knowledge to help you prevent and cope with emergencies. What you do with that knowledge is up to you.

2
WEATHER

Weather is an overworked topic of conversation, but it's still a subject of great significance to outdoorsmen. Lack of respect for weather plays a part in many outdoors disasters. High winds bring on boating accidents. Blizzards strand and freeze motorists and campers. Lightning and flashfloods claim many lives. Weather demands respect from outdoorsmen.

Take advantage of professional forecasts to avoid or prepare for dangerous weather conditions. Most large towns have National Weather Service offices. Talk to the local meteorologists to get up-to-date professional predictions.

An additional reliable source of weather information is a network of very high frequency (VHF) weather stations operated by the National Oceanic and Atmospheric Administration (NOAA). These stations were originally established along the seacoasts for boaters, but now about 90 percent of the United States population is within receiving range of a station.

VHF weather stations operate 24 hours a day, 365 days

a year. Weather messages for each station's immediate vicinity are repeated every 4 to 6 minutes and are revised at 2-hour intervals. A special receiver, carried by electronics shops and big sports stores, is needed to pick up these stations. For a list of VHF weather station locations, write to:

NOAA
National Weather Service
8060 13th Street
Silver Spring, MD 20910
Attn: W112

National Weather Service meteorologist Dave Williams cautions against confusing these professional forecasts with those on popular radio stations.

"Much of what you get on commercial stations is yesterday's material," Williams says. "Most disc jockeys just don't care. They use weather as a fill-in, and usually they doctor the language so the forecast doesn't say what we mean at all."

Meteorologists have standard terms with specific meanings. These are some of the more common:

1. *Ice storm or freezing rain.* Everything, including roads and highways, will be coated with ice. Don't drive.

2. *Snow.* Snow will be falling steadily.

3. *Heavy snow.* In 12 hours, 4 to 6 inches of snow will fall, or in 24 hours, more than 6 inches.

4. *Blizzard.* The temperature will be lower than 20° F., wind will be at least 35 miles an hour, and blowing or falling snow will cut visibility to one quarter mile or less.

5. *Cold wave.* The temperature will fall rapidly within 24 hours.

6. *Watch.* A winter storm or hurricane is approaching, or conditions are ideal for producing severe thunderstorms or tornadoes.

7. *Warning.* A winter storm or hurricane is about to hit,

or a severe thunderstorm or tornado is actually in progress.

Professional forecasts are updated regularly and are the most accurate available.

"But," Dave Williams points out, "they're still not 100 percent accurate. About the best accuracy we can achieve is 85 percent, so outdoorsmen must plan with that in mind."

In the backcountry, you may be unable to get professional information. Personal observation may be your only means of anticipating tough weather. Unsettled conditions such as a drop in temperature or unstable wind shifting back and forth may indicate an approaching storm. In winter, a dominant south wind can be particularly significant. According to Williams, *all winter storms in the northern hemisphere are preceded by a south wind.* He warns, however, that this may not be a reliable indicator everywhere. Topographic features in some localities prevent the wind's blowing from the south.

One predictable aspect of winter storms is a drastic drop in temperature during or after the storm.

Sometimes clouds may signal a brewing storm. Cirrus clouds, those high, sparse wisps often called "mares' tails," generally precede storm fronts. The old saying, "Red sky in morning, sailors' warning; red sky at night, sailors' delight," comes from this fact. Ice crystals in cirrus clouds diffuse early-morning sunlight to produce a red glow. However, cirrus clouds don't necessarily mean a storm is coming, nor is their absence proof that one isn't. Meteorologist Jim Rawles, a 25-year veteran with the National Weather Service, puts little faith in any cloud-based forecast.

"There are 27 different kinds of clouds," he says. "We can't even guess the weather from all our information. Can the layman look out and judge the weather from the looks of a particular cloud? Forget it. Simply beware of strange or unusual clouds, especially menacing-looking clouds. Big black clouds or other ominous cloud formations should tell you something."

In place of trying to forecast weather by atmospheric conditions, Rawles says outdoorsmen would be further ahead to learn local conditions and to prepare accordingly. Begin by investigating general geographic weather patterns. I frequently talk to people who come ill-prepared to visit my home state of Oregon. These visitors believe they'll find a mild, excessively rainy climate. Near the coast, where rainfall exceeds 100 inches a year, this impression is accurate. But inland, where two-thirds of the state is desert, conditions are harsh.

Before heading into the backcountry, don't be satisfied with such general knowledge. Boil it down more and learn specifics. When entering a new area, talk to gas-station people, forest rangers, local weathermen, old-timers, or anyone else who can offer insight. Isolated topographic localities may present unique hazards such as heavy, local fog or seasonal floods not found in surrounding country.

Winter Weather Dangers

Roughly, weather can be divided into two kinds— summer and winter. Winter weather involves storm systems that develop in the Arctic and over the oceans, then sweep long distances to the mainland United States, dropping rain or snow, bringing high winds and cold temperatures. In northern latitudes, these storms dominate weather patterns from October through May.

Winter storms can be long and severe. They may last a week or more, dumping several feet of snow, and the bitter temperatures that follow storms may seem endless. An added danger of winter storms, according to Dave Williams, is their potential surprise element.

"Storm fronts often travel 50 to 60 miles an hour," Williams says. "You can't rely on blue sky to promise good

Listen to professional weather forecasts before you set out on any outdoor activity. Then avoid getting so involved that you forget to check the sky periodically.

weather or on atmospheric signs to give warning. Winter storms move fast and can catch you unprepared. The weather picture in winter can change in a half hour."

The major threat to life in winter is exposure (covered fully in Chapter 3). Winter's moisture, wind, and cold are primary ingredients of exposure, and winter weather creates additional hazards that heighten the threat of exposure. Deep snows, as well as poor visibility from fog or falling snow, often strand winter travelers. Ice and snow increase the potential for accidents and injury. Cold temperatures and other aspects of winter activity drain a person's energy, accelerating fatigue and exhaustion. Outdoors survival in winter depends on an understanding of winter's special problems and the knowledge and preparation to handle them.

"Never underestimate the potential danger of what winter can throw at you," warns Bruce Wadlington of Crater Lake National Park, a popular winter sports area. "Too often people look at the clear sky and take off for a 3-day ski trip with a minimum of equipment, apparently never thinking about where the 20 feet of snow on the ground came from. Always carry a good tent for shelter. And if you plan to tour for 2 days, take provisions for 4. Go prepared for the worst."

In addition, Wadlington says, outdoorsmen should always travel with companions in winter, and every party should have an experienced member.

"Winter camping presents special problems," he stresses. "Setting up a tent is much harder on snow than on dry ground. Staying dry in snow or rain is a chore. The cold of winter saps your strength and energy. Someone in the party should have solid experience in dealing with these obstacles. Winter camping resembles scuba diving in important ways. You don't just get a pair of tanks and dive by yourself. You go with somebody who knows how until you learn the ropes."

Wadlington suggests that if you don't have an experienced winter-camping friend, you should practice camping—first by setting up a few yards off the road and staying out a night, then by doing the same thing a couple of miles further in from the road. Then if things do go wrong, you can reach safety. If your first winter-camping emergency comes 10 miles from the nearest road, you could be in serious trouble.

Before taking longer outings, also get experience that will help you to assess your physical capabilities.

"For example," Wadlington has observed, "novice skiers commonly overestimate their own abilities. They set out

Winter camping makes heavy demands on your skill and your equipment. Practice under safe conditions before you head into the backcountry.

On snow or water, too much sun is a possible hazard. Zinc-oxide ointment on lips, nose, and other sensitive areas may look funny, but it can prevent sunburn and avoid a wrecked trip.

Snowblindness can be a threat, so adequate eye protection is a must. Sunglasses should wrap around or have side shields to keep out ultraviolet rays reflected from the snow.

when the snow is packed, and they can ski 5 or 6 miles an hour. It's fun. But the next day a storm dumps 8 inches of new snow. That's when they find out what tough going really means. Skiing fresh snow is hard work. Find out how good you are before heading into the backcountry."

Snowshoeing presents little danger of injury since just about anyone who can walk can snowshoe safely. Skis are a different matter. You can lose control. Sprains, shoulder separations, and head injuries are among the common skiing injuries. The time to test your ability and to push yourself is during practice sessions where help is at hand. In the backcountry, ski conservatively and under control.

One serious danger that you should be alert for in mountain country is avalanches. An avalanche is a snow slide that occurs when unstable surface snow, either a slab or deep powder, slides on a smooth base. Early winter storms create little avalanche danger because rocks and logs anchor the snow. But with succeeding storms, anchor points are covered. A smooth runway develops, and new snow can slide downhill easily.

Generally, avalanche danger increases with each new snowfall. The danger decreases in a day or two as the snow settles and consolidates. Weight is a triggering element for avalanches, so the greater a new snowfall is, the greater the avalanche danger it presents.

Wind also magnifies avalanche potential. During a high wind, snow accumulates rapidly on leeward slopes, often forming a crusty slab of snow that will slide readily. Also during a wind, tons of snow can build up at the tops of ridges to form cornices, which can crumble under their own weight to start avalanches. Avoid steep, leeward slopes during and soon after storms.

Any moderate-to-steep open slope can have an avalanche. Long slopes are generally more dangerous than short slopes since snow can develop greater weight and momentum there, but short slopes can be hazardous, too.

"People have been buried by avalanches on slopes no

more than 15 or 20 feet long," Bruce Wadlington says. "A heavy slab can run right over the top of you, and it doesn't take much snow to bury a person."

Be particularly suspicious of open chutes in heavy timber. Most likely the chute is bare because avalanches continually wipe out the trees there.

If you're in avalanche country, pick your travel route carefully. Scott Heywood—who teaches mountain climbing and winter safety to interested citizens in the Bighorn Mountains of Wyoming—advises traveling the tops of ridges above danger areas. If that's not possible, he says, stay out on the flat of a valley, away from the bottom of steep slopes. The most dangerous route, he says, is across the middle of a slope.

"Most avalanches aren't acts of God," Heywood explains. "People trigger them by adding weight to the snow field and by creating a fracture line in slab snow. If you must travel an avalanche slope, do it vertically. You don't create a fracture line that way."

If for some reason a person is forced to cross a dangerous slope, he should attach and string out an avalanche cord—a bright nylon line 50 or more feet long that can be seen on the surface of the snow and traced to the buried victim. He should wear mittens, cap, and coat to provide warmth if trapped under the snow, and he should remove ski-pole straps from around his wrists and remove ski safety straps. He should also loosen his pack and other equipment so he can shed as much weight and bulk as possible if he is caught in a slide. And if he is swept into an avalanche, he should, according to Bruce Wadlington, get into a fetal position, drawing his knees to his chest.

"With muscles contracted, you can push to make an air space or to break through to the surface," Wadlington explains. "If you're laid out flat with your entire body surface covered by snow, you can't move."

Only one person at a time should cross a slope. Others

in the party should stay in a protected site and watch. If an individual is caught, those watching should follow his progress and mark the spot he was seen last. When the slide has stopped, companions of the victim should begin searching immediately. An avalanche victim is unlikely to survive under the snow more than a couple of hours. Going to find help would normally take longer than that. As Wadlington puts it, "By the time rescue crews arrive, they won't be searching to save a life. They'll be looking for a body. The victim's only hope is his companions."

Summer Weather Dangers

Excessive heat is a primary danger in summer. As temperatures rise into the 90s and above, staying cool is as big a problem as staying warm is in winter. Heatstroke and heat exhaustion, life-threatening results of summer heat, are covered fully in Chapter 4.

Heat, though, isn't the only threatening element of summer weather. Storms are also cause for concern. In contrast to winter storms, which travel long distances, summer storms are spawned locally. As the sun warms air near the earth's surface, the warm moisture-laden air rises. At the colder high altitudes, the moisture condenses into visible water droplets, forming a cloud. Through a complex physical process, the cloud builds into a thunderhead, sometimes rising as high as 40,000 feet. When this cloud has matured, heavy rain or hail begins to fall, and a cold downdraft produces strong wind beneath the cloud.

The thunderstorm season generally runs from June through September, although in Southern states it's much longer. Summer storms generally lack the surprise element and longevity of winter storms. Normally, they build gradually within view and often die out in less than an hour. What they lack in speed and duration, however, they can make up in violence.

One fearful aspect of summer storms is lightning. Lightning annually kills more people in the United States than any other aspect of weather. One federal agency puts the yearly average death rate by lightning at 125; another says it's 600. Whatever the exact number, the potential danger is clear.

Lightning is electricity. Thunderclouds carry a powerful negative electrical charge, and a positive charge builds up in the earth beneath the cloud. As these charges attract each other, the positive earth charge follows the cloud, flowing upward toward the cloud through high objects such as buildings, trees, and hilltops. However, air is a poor conductor of electricity, so these charges are unable to break loose until they become powerful enough to overcome the air's resistanc. When they finally do, they've built up tremendous power, producing a charge of up to 15,000,000 volts. Lightning is produced when the charges come together. The heat of lightning can equal that of the sun's surface. This great heat causes an explosive expansion of air, producing the popping and rumbling we know as thunder.

Sound travels through the air approximately 1 mile every 5 seconds, so you can judge the distance and travel direction of a thunderstorm. If you count 10 seconds from the time you see lightning until you hear thunder, you know the storm is about 2 miles away. If successive counts get shorter, the storm is heading your way.

The safest shelter during a lightning storm is a building or car. If lightning hits these, the electricity flows through the walls or car body into the ground, offering you nearly 100 percent protection.

If you're caught outdoors, stay away from prominent features such as tall trees or poles and the tops of peaks or ridges. The ground charge flows up through these, making them potential strike points. The best place to be is among low trees or brush, well below the top of a ridge. A cave is a good place to wait out a storm. If you're caught in the open, lie down in a ditch or depression to get as low as possible.

Avoid wire fences, railroad tracks, metal pipes, or other good conductors of electricity. If you're on or in the water, get to shore. Water is a good conductor, so a lightning strike on the water, even some distance away, can kill you.

Lightning kills by electrocution. When a person is hit, the electricity short-circuits body functions. Cause of death is normally respiratory failure. First aid is artificial respiration.

Another deadly product of thunderstorms is flash-floods, which claim an average of 100 lives a year in the United States. Rainfall from thunderstorms can be so heavy, often several inches in a few hours, that the ground can't absorb it. It runs off in rivulets and streams that accumulate to form a torrent.

A thunderstorm doesn't have to be in your immediate vicinity to hit you with a flood. A storm several miles upstream can send a wall of water onto you. During the thunderstorm season, place your camp on high ground, not in draws or creek beds. And stay away from streams and rivers that are rising rapidly.

In particular, stay off flooded roads. In the Southwest, where flashfloods are common, many roads cross dry washes. Motorists who've tried to cross these during thunderstorms have been swept several miles downstream and found dead, days later. Water washing over the road can be swifter and deeper than it seems, and it can be rising fast. Stop and wait until the water recedes before crossing a flooded dip.

A third danger from thunderstorms is tornadoes, which are whirling columns of air. These are the most violent and destructive of all storms. The Environmental Science

Services Administration says about 600 tornadoes hit the United States each year, killing an average of 125 people annually. Tornadoes have occurred in all 50 states, but they're more frequent in some regions than others. The Central states are considered the tornado belt. Texas, Oklahoma, Kansas, and Nebraska report the highest average number of tornadoes each year.

The tornado season begins in February along the Gulf of Mexico and moves northward and westward with the coming of summer. About half the total number of tornadoes will occur in April, May, and June. Tornadoes may develop at any time of day, but they are most common during late afternoon. Warm, humid, unstable air breeds tornadoes.

A tornado looks like a thin column extending down from the base of a thundercloud. It may be white or gray toward the top but black near the bottom because of debris and dirt swept from the earth. The noise has been described as that of 10 jet airplanes or 100 train engines.

Wind velocity in a tornado may reach 300 miles an hour. The danger is mainly from getting thrown about or hit by flying objects. At home, the safest place is in the basement or under solidly built-in benches or cabinets. If you are caught outdoors, move at a right angle to the approaching tornado to get out of its path, which is usually no more than ¼ mile wide. If you can't get out of the way, lie in a depression or ravine, as low and flat as possible.

3

EXPOSURE

Exposure is a general word referring to problems caused by cold. Exposure in itself is not an injury. It's the condition that leads to injuries. The most severe injuries caused by exposure are hypothermia and frostbite. These two conditions result from similar processes, so a look at the effects of exposure in general helps to understand hypothermia and frostbite.

In a person suffering from exposure, heat is drained away faster than the body can produce and replace it. This excessive heat loss occurs in five ways:

• **Respiration** is the least preventable. Cold air inhaled into the lungs uses body heat to warm it. This heat is carried away when the air is exhaled. Respiration accounts for significant heat loss. You can reduce it to some degree by regulating physical activity. You'll thereby avoid panting and the inhalation of huge quantities of cold air.

• **Radiation** accounts for considerable heat loss. Blood vessels transport heat from the central body to the skin. Here the heat radiates into the air, much as it does from hot pavement in summer, creating heat waves. Loss of body heat through radiation is especially rapid in the

Air temperature doesn't have to be subfreezing or even freezing to cause hypothermia. Moderate temperature in combination with wet and wind can be deadly. These houndmen must stay alert to conditions in order to avoid trouble.

By paying close attention to the level of your activity and the way you're dressed (the layer system is readily adjustable) you can avoid sweating and the resultant chilling.

hands and feet, the groin, armpits, and head where vessels lie close to the surface. Adequate clothing preserves radiated heat.

• **Evaporation** is a third means of cooling the body. Moisture evaporating on the skin draws heat from the body. In hot weather this is a life-saving cooling process. But in cold weather it can be deadly. Whether you get wet from rain, sweat, or falling into a creek makes no difference. All water has the same effect. The only protection against excessive cooling by evaporation is to stay dry.

• **Convection** is another robber of body heat. A breeze or wind is a convection current, and it carries away heat faster than does calm air. In calm air, clothing traps body heat and keeps you warm. But a brisk wind blowing through your clothing sweeps away this warmth and chills you quickly. Windproof garments and shelter from wind are vital in preventing heat loss by convection.

• **Conduction** is the fifth means of heat loss. Conduction is the transfer of heat from one substance to another. For example, if you pick up a metal tent stake, heat passes from your hand to the stake. If you sit directly on snow, some of your heat is conducted into the snow. This loss is prevented by insulation, say by gloves or a foam sleeping pad.

Certain conditions make these five cooling processes particularly threatening. Cold, of course, is one. The colder the air temperature, the greater the potential for chilling.

Equally significant is wind. Through convection, wind chills exposed skin quickly. This accelerated cooling rate is called the chill factor. On a calm day, a 40° F. temperature may seem comfortable. Yet if that same temperature is coupled with a 20-mile-per-hour wind, the resulting chill factor is equal to that of calm 20° F. air. The accompanying chart indicates the chilling rates for various combinations of temperature and wind. As you see, chill factor, not just air temperature, is of great concern.

WIND SPEED		COOLING POWER OF WIND EXPRESSED AS "EQUIVALENT CHILL TEMPERATURE"																					
KNOTS	MPH	TEMPERATURE (°F)																					
CALM	CALM	40	35	30	25	20	15	10	5	0	-5	-10	-15	-20	-25	-30	-35	-40	-45	-50	-55	-60
		EQUIVALENT CHILL TEMPERATURE																					
3-6	5	35	30	25	20	15	10	5	0	-5	-10	-15	-20	-25	-30	-35	-40	-45	-50	-55	-65	-70
7-10	10	30	20	15	10	5	0	-10	-15	-20	-25	-35	-40	-45	-50	-60	-65	-70	-75	-80	-90	-95
11-15	15	25	15	10	0	-5	-10	-20	-25	-30	-40	-45	-50	-60	-65	-70	-80	-85	-90	-100	-105	-110
16-19	20	20	10	5	0	-10	-15	-25	-30	-35	-45	-50	-60	-65	-75	-80	-85	-95	-100	-110	-115	-120
20-23	25	15	10	0	-5	-15	-20	-30	-35	-45	-50	-60	-65	-75	-80	-90	-95	-105	-110	-120	-125	-135
24-28	30	10	5	0	-10	-20	-25	-30	-40	-50	-55	-65	-70	-80	-85	-95	-100	-110	-115	-125	-130	-140
29-32	35	10	5	-5	-10	-20	-30	-35	-40	-50	-60	-65	-75	-80	-90	-100	-105	-115	-120	-130	-135	-145
33-36	40	10	0	-5	-15	-20	-30	-35	-45	-55	-60	-70	-75	-85	-95	-100	-110	-115	-125	-130	-140	-150
WINDS ABOVE 40 HAVE LITTLE ADDITIONAL EFFECT.		LITTLE DANGER				INCREASING DANGER (Flesh may freeze within 1 minute)							GREAT DANGER (Flesh may freeze within 30 seconds)									

DANGER OF FREEZING EXPOSED FLESH FOR PROPERLY CLOTHED PERSONS

This chart shows the extent to which winds of various velocities contribute to chilling. You must have adequate protection against wind in order to avoid hypothermia and frostbite.

Moisture accelerates cooling through evaporation and by destroying the insulative ability of clothing. Even more significant, water is an excellent conductor, carrying away heat many times faster than air. For this reason, immersion in cold water is a critical danger. For example, barring the complications of wind or wet clothing, 50° F. air won't chill a well-clothed person. If, however, that person is immersed in 50° F. water, he'll die from loss of body heat in less than 3 hours. In 32° F. water, he'll last only about 1½ hours.

These figures come to me from John S. Hayward, a Ph. D. in the Department of Biology at the University of Victoria, British Columbia, Canada. Dr. Hayward has been involved in extensive studies on hypothermia. In addition to assuring me that these data are the most reliable available on hypothermia, he had some additional observations and comments on the subject.

"The figures for 32-degree F. water," he said, "were extrapolated from experimental findings for water of higher temperature, about 39 degrees F. So the 1½ hours for 32-degree water may be a little long. But death from hypothermia would certainly never occur in less than one hour.

"There is a great myth about cold water. The survival time is longer than most people think. Much of what you hear about someone's dying of hypothermia in 5 or 10 minutes is just folklore. Once in a while, a person dies very rapidly, but it's not from hypothermia. It may be from one of various shock responses. A person may hyperventilate and become unconscious or may inhale water and drown. And of course people may get stiff and be unable to hold onto the ice or the boat or whatever else they're hanging onto. So they drown. But deaths that occur in a matter of minutes are not from hypothermia. People have simply misinterpreted what the cause of death was."

Hayward goes on to say that his figures are based on experimental studies in which a number of people were placed in water of about 39 degrees F. (4½ degrees C.). He says he personally was in that water for 40 minutes. In that time, his core body temperature dropped from 99 to 95 degrees. He was remaining still, and he was wearing a life preserver and lightweight clothing.

"For our experiments we figured the point of death at a core body temperature of about 85 degrees F. (30 degrees C.). That's really very lenient because the actual point of death, when a person's heart stops," he says, "generally is below 80 degrees F. Figuring the point of death at 85 degrees F., in 40 minutes I was only 'one-third' of the way to death.

"Our data on the progression of hypothermia are based on the core body temperature taken rectally, not on subjective observations and feelings such as shivering, how cold a person feels, or how he looks. Although skin temperature plunges instantly, it takes 10 to 15 minutes in even the coldest water for the core temperature to drop at all. When it does begin to fall, the rate of cooling is linear (that is, it progresses at a steady rate rather than accelerating), but the rate of cooling varies depending on water temperature. The colder the water, the faster the rate of deep-body cooling."

It's important to note that the survival rates are figured for a person remaining still. People in the experiments wore flotation devices, so they didn't have to swim or tread water to stay afloat. This flotation factor is significant. As Hayward points out, the UVic studies have shown that swimming or other physical activity increases the cooling rate by about 35 percent. In other words, if the survival time for a person who remains still in 32-degree F. water is 1½ hours, it would be only one hour if he were swimming.

Moisture in clothing, when cooled to air temperature of 50° F., has a cooling effect similar to that of deep water of that temperature. That's one reason staying dry is critically important.

"If you're covered with damp, perspiration-soaked clothes it's the same thing as being immersed in cold water," says Dr. Everett Howard, an Oregon internist and expert mountain climber. "The first thing to do is to take off those damp clothes and to get the victim into some dry clothes. Get him out of the water. That's the first thing you'd do if you saw a man in a lake. You'd get him out of the water."

Clothing is the chief ingredient in the prevention of chilling from cold, wind, and moisture. Chapter 6 covers this subject thoroughly, but the major points in relation to exposure are worth emphasizing here.

First, wear wool. It provides some insulation even when wet. When you're exerting yourself, shed heavy clothes to avoid getting soaked by sweat; during rests, put on warm clothing to halt chilling. Don rain gear before you get wet and wind gear before you begin to chill from the wind. Give special attention to areas of greatest heat loss. Wear a wool hat and scarf to protect the vital neck and head. Wear adequate gloves and footgear. While resting, sit with your arms against your sides and pull your legs against your chest to reduce radiated heat loss from the armpits and groin.

Remember also that internal factors contribute to cold injury. Dehydration, by inhibiting circulation, lowers resistance to cold. To prevent dehydration, drink plenty of liquid throughout the day. Unless absolutely necessary, don't eat ice and snow, which rob you of valuable energy as they melt and get warm in the stomach. If possible, drink hot liquids.

Fatigue adds to the effects of exposure by depleting energy reserves and slowing muscle activity, thus lessening the body's ability to produce heat. Eat high-energy foods regularly, and regulate physical activity to avoid exhaustion.

Hypothermia

Hypo- is a Greek word meaning "under" or "less than the ordinary," and *thermia* means "heat." Hypothermia, then, means less than ordinary heat, that is, lower than normal body temperature.

Your central, or core, body temperature is normally about 99° F. For the heart, lungs, brain, and other vital organs to function properly this temperature must remain nearly constant. Hypothermia is the condition in which core temperature drops. Life-sustaining processes slow down, and if the temperature falls far enough, they stop.

Imagine a person who has been drenched by a sudden rainstorm. As wind, evaporation, and conduction cool his skin, blood vessels to the skin and muscles constrict to reduce blood flow there. This is a normal, protective mechanism to reduce radiated heat loss through the skin. In essence, the body is sacrificing the extremities to preserve warmth for the vital organs. Skin temperature may drop as much as 40 to 50° F. while the core temperature remains nearly normal.

If cooling of the extremities isn't reversed, eventually the central body temperature itself begins to drop. As cooling progresses, the body goes through several stages. These can vary, but they follow a general pattern. As the core temperature drops 2 or 3° F., uncontrollable shivering begins. Shivering is an involuntary muscular action to generate heat. If the shivering fails to create enough heat to offset heat loss, body temperature continues sliding. Below 95° F., shivering continues but thinking dulls and speech is slurred. If body temperature falls below 90° F., shivering ceases and the muscles become rigid. The victim's movements become erratic, and he's disoriented. At 85° F., the victim becomes irrational and stuporous. Below 80° F., he falls into coma and dies.

Recognizing symptoms is critical in preventing death from hypothermia. Lee Juillerat, an experienced outdoorsman, has witnessed several cases of hypothermia during various climbs on Mt. Shasta, California. In one instance a man with a normally deep, calm voice started talking erratically in squealy tones. On another occasion, Juillerat noticed signs of stress and fatigue on a companion's face.

"As I went over a small rise," Juillerat relates, "he was right behind me. When he didn't show up for several minutes, I went back to look for him. He'd barely moved. He simply was going much slower than fatigue alone warranted, and he stuttered when he talked. He was hypothermic and had to be warmed before we could go on."

Irrational thought, apathy, and uncontrollable shivering are other symptoms of hypothermia.

One big danger of hypothermia is that a person often doesn't recognize symptoms in himself. Dropping body temperature affects thinking in such a way that a victim simply can't observe his own condition objectively.

"Rarely will a hypothermic person admit anything is wrong," Juillerat stresses. "I saw a typical example while climbing Mt. Shasta in California. A woman started giggling and talking irrationally. She acted as if she'd been drinking martinis, but she insisted, 'I'm not cold, I'm not cold.'

"We finally made her sit down and huddled around to warm her up. As she began to rewarm, she suddenly realized how extremely cold she'd been. That scared her badly."

Because of hypothermia's insidious nature, members of a party should watch each other closely for developing signs.

"And," Juillerat suggests, "you should always accept another person's judgment. He can see signs that you can't see in yourself."

If you're alone, the burden is wholly on you. Allow a wide margin of safety by building good shelter and utilizing adequate clothing in any threatening conditions. Never ignore shivering or fatigue. If even the slightest signs appear, bivouac or set up camp immediately and get warm.

The major danger of hypothermia is that once a person's core temperature has dropped to about 95° F., he can no longer rewarm himself. Only with the help of an external heat source can his temperature be raised to normal. Once inner cooling has begun, it can progress rapidly. Time from initial symptoms to death may be less than 2 hours. Therefore, treatment must be immediate.

First, prevent continued heat loss by getting the victim out of the wind or rain and removing all wet clothing.

Subsequent measures will depend on circumstances. If you're no more than a few minutes' drive from home, the ideal treatment is to place the victim in a tub of 110° F. water. Arms and legs should be kept out of the water initially so the blood won't rush to these extremities, which would lower the blood pressure to vital organs. The central body should be warmed first.

In the backcountry, where hot baths are scarce, other methods must do. Under most conditions, the best way to rewarm a person is body-to-body contact. Strip the victim of clothing and get him into a sleeping bag, or roll him in blankets with another person, also stripped. If the bag is large enough, two or more people should surround the victim. The more skin contact, the quicker the rewarming. Above all, remember that putting the victim in a sleeping bag by himself, or dressing him warmly, will do no good. Sleeping bags and heavy clothes don't produce heat. They just preserve it. The hypothermic victim is producing little or no heat, so he'll continue to freeze unless warmed externally.

A valuable part of treatment, if the person is conscious, is to give him hot drinks. These go straight to the core body, where heat is needed most.

If you're caught without a sleeping bag, at least seek protection. Make a good wind break. Build a fire if possible, or use your stove to heat liquids. Again, huddle close to the victim to give him external warmth.

Frostbite

Frostbite, another product of exposure, is the destruction of tissue through freezing. Although it's most common among mountain climbers and Arctic travelers where high altitude and extreme cold exaggerate body cooling, frostbite can occur in any cold weather. Air doesn't have to be subfreezing.

Poor circulation is the chief condition leading to frostbite. The hands, feet, ears, nose, and face—which are most exposed and where circulation is first impaired under cold conditions—are affected first and most severely. Because general body cooling automatically constricts vessels in these parts, warm clothing for the body as well as the extremities is essential in preventing frostbite.

Of special importance, clothing must not be constrictive. A windbreaker with tight elastic on the wrists cuts circulation to the hands. Knickers tight at the knees reduce circulation in the feet. Wear loose clothing, and do other things to enhance circulation. In particular, loosen your boots at rest breaks, and, around camp, wear loose-fitting slippers or shoes to promote circulation in the feet.

Often snow is much colder underneath than at the surface. On rest breaks, raise your feet into the warmer air above the snow. If, on the other hand, your boots are damp or the wind is blowing, you may be better off to keep your feet in the snow and out of the air where evaporation and wind chill will be greater.

Avoid chilling by conduction. Sit on a pad or pack to keep off the snow or frozen ground. Wear gloves to pick up metal objects, which can freeze the skin quickly. And be especially careful with stove fuels. Gasoline evaporates with a speed that, in cold weather, can cause instant frostbite.

Smoking and drinking are poor practices in cold weather. Smoking constricts blood vessels, inhibiting circulation. Alcohol, besides fogging a person's thinking, dilates vessels, thereby promoting excessive cooling.

In any cold weather, constantly be aware of any severe chilling. Often affected parts will be painful, but sometimes they may not be. Use the buddy system to watch each other for signs of frost nip, especially on the face and cheeks, where you can't see it yourself. The skin will turn an ashy white. Warm a frost-nipped cheek by applying steady, direct pressure with a warm hand. If fingers are chilled, tuck them under your armpits. Put chilled feet against a friend's stomach or in his armpits. Such treatment, however, should be used only with superficial chilling.

If tissue actually has frozen, special treatment is required. You can recognize frozen tissue by its white, yellow-white, or blotchy-blue color. It will be firm and insensitive. Normally, if a part of the body hurts severely from cold and then suddenly goes numb, it has frozen.

In most cases, frostbite should not be treated in the field. For one thing, after frostbitten areas are rewarmed, the victim can become a stretcher case. If his feet are affected, he can't walk. The pain will be too severe. Besides, walking will cause permanent damage.

Equally serious is the potential for refreezing. Dr. Everett Howard explains:

"As frozen tissue thaws, the cells weep and fluid collects between them. If the tissue is then refrozen, the fluid forms ice crystals between the cells. These crystals may cause extensive, irreparable damage."

On the other hand, since frozen flesh is numb, a person with frozen feet can walk some distance to get himself to safety. And, according to Dr. Howard, many cases have been recorded where hands and feet, frozen for several days, have been thawed under ideal conditions with no lasting damage.

Treatment should begin only when conditions are such that the patient won't have to move under his own power and where refreezing is not a possibility. The ideal place for treatment and aftercare is the hospital.

If for some reason hospitalization isn't possible, the frozen part should be treated by the rapid rewarming method. This is done by immersing the frozen area in water (carrying a small thermometer is a wise idea) between 100 and 112° F., no hotter. Fred T. Darvill, Jr., M.D., in his booklet "Mountaineering Medicine, A Wilderness Medical Guide," says: "However, in a crisis, one can test the water temperature by immersion of a normal hand. The water should be comfortably warm but should not burn the test hand."

The frozen area should be kept in the water only until sensation and color return throughout the frozen part. The affected area may turn deep purple, and large, clear blisters, called blebs, will develop. This is a normal, good sign.

Proper treatment after rewarming is also critical. After-care is aimed primarily at preventing infection. Blisters should never be broken. The affected area should be immobilized and kept in a sterile surrounding. Even contact with sheets can be damaging, so a frostbitten limb should be supported to prevent contact with any surface. Frostbite rarely causes permanent damage if proper care is administered for several weeks until new skin has replaced the old.

Tissue destruction and amputation result from improper treatment. One such improper treatment is thawing frozen skin by exposure to intense heat such as an open fire or excessively hot water. Excessive heat literally cooks the flesh and kills it.

Equally destructive is the practice of rubbing with ice, snow, or cold water. Such treatment makes no more sense than treating a burn with hotpacks.

Allowing frostbite to thaw slowly and spontaneously as the victim enters a warmer environment also can result in severe damage. Also, rubbing an affected area destroys cells. Never rub frozen skin.

To summarize: the best treatment for frostbite is rapid thawing in water of 100 to 112° F., with sterile aftercare.

4

HOT-WEATHER

DANGERS

The internal body operates no more efficiently at an abnormally high temperature than at a lower-than-normal temperature. For this reason, hot weather presents temperature-regulating problems as serious as those caused by cold weather.

The same mechanisms that cause excessive cooling in winter are necessary for adequate cooling in summer. Although little can be done to alter the rate of heat exchange through respiration, much can be done to enhance cooling through the four other processes: radiation, evaporation, convection, and conduction.

You can encourage radiation of excess body heat by drinking plenty of liquids to maintain good circulation.

You can sprinkle water on your skin or swim in cold water to allow evaporation and conduction to cool you.

You can wear loose clothing and rest in breezy spots so heat will be swept away by convection.

These are only examples. The point is, those same processes that *threaten life in winter* must be put to use to *save life in summer*.

Heatstroke

Heatstroke, sometimes called sunstroke, is the most serious hot-weather problem. It can kill a person within minutes, and heatstroke deaths aren't uncommon. A July newspaper headline reads: "Texas Heat Wave Kills 21 Persons." Heatstroke caused these deaths as the temperature rose above 100° F. for 17 straight days. Ed Little, who worked for a Los Angeles County search-and-rescue unit for many years, said hikers frequently fell victim to heatstroke in the Los Angeles hills.

If you know how the body cools itself, you're better able to understand heatstroke. The circulatory system is the body's cooling system. Blood flows through the heart, lungs, and other vital organs and picks up excess heat. The blood transports this heat to the skin, where the heat radiates into the air.

When the excess-heat load becomes too great for circulating blood alone to handle, the sweating mechanism comes into action. In effect, sweating simply covers the body with water. This water evaporates, reduces skin temperature, and cools the body.

Under extreme conditions, even the sweating process is unable to handle the heat load. When this happens, core body temperature begins to rise. If it rises far enough, the sweating mechanism is knocked out. Body temperature skyrockets, and the result is heatstroke.

Heatstroke occurs in two ways:

• One is overexertion. A person's working muscles generate heat. In hot weather, the exercising muscles may create heat faster than the cooling system can get rid of it, raising the core body temperature. Exertional heatstroke is most likely in an unconditioned person who overworks in hot conditions, but it threatens anyone engaged in prolonged hot-weather exertion.

• The other, classic heatstroke, is caused by high air temperature alone. A person doesn't necessarily have to

In desert country, beware of heatstroke. Carry plenty of water, drink some of it regularly, and avoid overexertion.

be exercising. If the air surrounding the body is hotter than normal body temperature, it potentially can reverse the effects of the cooling system. The blood, instead of dispersing excess body heat into the air, carries higher-than-body-temperature heat from the air to the core body, raising body temperature. Classic heatstroke most often fells the elderly, people with chronic illness, and alcoholics.

Certain conditions are responsible for heatstroke. High air temperature, in the 90s and above, leads to overheating in a couple of ways. For one thing, it causes dehydration through heavy sweating. Also, the hotter the air, the less quickly the heat can radiate from the body. If the air is hotter than body temperature, heat can't radiate at all.

That's when sweating is essential for cooling. But,

atmospheric conditions can reduce the effectiveness of sweating. High humidity decreases the rate of evaporation. Although you may seem to sweat more heavily in humid weather than in dry, you actually don't. The difference is that sweat doesn't evaporate as rapidly in humid weather. It just runs off in streams and is wasted. Only by evaporating can sweat cool you.

Calm air also aggravates overheating. A breeze evaporates sweat quickly, but in calm air the process is slow.

In any hot weather, particularly when humidity is high and the air is calm, do everything possible to prevent overheating. Since water is the vital ingredient in the body's cooling system, the drinking of adequate liquid is the critical preventive measure. However, saving water in your canteen does no good if you're already sweating heavily. You're still dehydrating. The only way to conserve water is to decrease fluid loss, that is, to slow down and rest so you'll sweat less. For hot-weather outings, allow at least a gallon of water per person daily, and drink some regularly.

Pure water is probably the best drink. To be of value, liquids must be absorbed into the bloodstream quickly. Liquids such as sodas with high sugar content are absorbed slowly.

Hot-weather clothing should be lightweight and loose fitting to allow for air circulation. White or light-colored clothing reflects sunlight for better cooling. Wear a brimmed hat to keep direct sunlight off your head.

Limit your activity in hot weather, especially if you're out of condition. Don't push yourself. Rest frequently in the shade or in a cool building to allow your body to get rid of excess heat.

Finally, learn the symptoms of heatstroke, and watch for them in yourself and others. According to Ed Little, during his time with a Los Angeles search-and-rescue unit, many people died because companions of the victims didn't know the signs of heatstroke. In most cases, they believed the problem to be a heart attack and so failed to give first aid even though water, the only resource needed to save the victim's life, was close at hand.

In the *early* stages of heatstroke, a person sweats profusely, becomes irritable, and shows signs of fatigue. He may have a throbbing pressure in the head or a severe headache, unsteadiness, dizziness, and nausea. He may chill.

When the body temperature nears 105° F., he'll collapse. The skin probably will be hot, red, and dry. Dry skin indicates that sweating has ceased and is a positive sign of heatstroke. However, a person suffering exertional heatstroke may still be sweating upon collapse, so don't wait for dry skin before you begin treatment. Any time a person collapses in hot weather, treat for heatstroke. Once sweating has stopped, the body temperature may rise within minutes to 108 to 110° F. At that temperature, the victim will die, so treatment must be immediate.

The body temperature must be lowered quickly. Ideal treatment is to put the victim in a tub of ice water. When that's not possible, which it almost never will be in the outdoors, move the victim into the shade, strip off his clothes, and pour water over his entire body. Then fan him vigorously. Fanning increases the rate of evaporation for faster cooling. Apply more water and continue fanning until body temperature returns to normal. A heatstroke victim should be kept out of sunlight and heat for several weeks after recovery. A victim of heatstroke should see a doctor as soon as possible.

Heat Exhaustion

Heat exhaustion, or heat prostration, is caused by dehydration when a person sweats heavily and doesn't replace lost fluids. This condition may develop in a matter of hours if the difference between fluid loss and intake is great.

It also may develop over a period of days. During strenuous hot-weather activity, a person can't drink enough to replace all lost fluid immediately. He must drink more than usual for several hours after exertion to bring body fluids back to normal. If he resumes exercise before all fluids are replaced, water loss can be cumulative, leading eventually to heat exhaustion. For this reason, drinking as much water as possible, both during and after activity, is the essential preventive measure.

Symptoms of heat exhaustion are weakness and fatigue, irritability, headache, dizziness, and—possibly—vomiting. The victim's skin will be pale, cool, and clammy with sweat, and his temperature will be normal (in heatstroke, the skin is hot, red and dry, and temperature is high).

Treat heat exhaustion as shock. Get the victim into the shade. Lay him on his back, head level with the body, and feet elevated 10 or 12 inches. Have him drink slightly salted water (½ to 1 teaspoon of salt to a pint or two large glasses of water) slowly, about one glass every half hour. Don't force drinking if he vomits. Keep him cool with wet cloths or water sprinkled over his body. After recovery, a victim of heat exhaustion should rest and stay out of the heat for at least a day.

Heat Cramps and Salt Tablets

Sometimes cramps strike muscles that have been in hard use for several hours, such as the large leg muscles used during hiking. The muscles will twitch and then tighten into a painful knot. Heat cramps cause no permanent damage but can be debilitating for a while. Prevention and treatment simply involves an adequate intake of salt and water.

The cause of heat cramps seems to be questionable.

Some authorities say cramps result solely from salt depletion. Others say dehydration itself, as much as salt loss, is to blame.

That raises the question: Should you take salt tablets? Some doctors and writers say without reservation to take salt tablets in hot weather. They recommend two or three 1-gram coated tablets a day. Coated tablets dissolve in the intestine; plain tablets dissolve in the stomach and can cause nausea.

Doctors I've talked to say salt tablets are rarely, if ever, needed. Dr. Everett Howard says:

"Salt is necessary for strength. When you lose excessive salt, your muscles become very weak. With average hiking this is no problem. You get plenty of salt with your ordinary diet. If you're sweating badly, you can lose salt, leading to cramps and weakness. But that's easy to take care of—just salt your meals a little heavier than normal. I wouldn't give salt tablets a serious thought unless I were really sweating under extreme conditions. Too much salt can cause other problems."

Outdoorsman and marathon runner Dr. Alden Glidden says:

"If you're eating a normal diet, you need no extra salt. All food contains salt, and your body stores a great amount of salt. Salt tablets aren't needed under ordinary conditions. If you're getting no food or are on a salt-restricted diet and loss of salt through sweating is abnormal, there may be a need for supplemental salt."

5

DEHYDRATION
AND FATIGUE

Rarely does a person who is healthy and adequately rested suffer injuries from cold or heat. These and other problems usually overcome people who are weakened or sensitized by added complications. Probably the two main contributing elements to outdoors injuries are dehydration and fatigue.

Dehydration

Water is vital for survival. Without water under exhausting or hot conditions, a person may die of dehydration within 2 or 3 days. Dehydration is rarely that severe, but even in moderate degrees, dehydration can contribute to other problems that threaten your survival.

Dehydration occurs when a person loses more fluids than he takes in. Under average conditions, a person loses about 2 quarts of liquids per day. Half of this is lost through urination, the other half through sweating and through evaporation from the lungs. Under abnormal conditions, fluid loss can be double that amount or more. In hot weather, greatest loss is to sweating. In cold weather, sweating can be heavy and evaporation from the lungs can be significant, particularly at high altitudes where the air is dry. Severe diarrhea and vomiting also can cause dehydration.

Under any of these circumstances, a person must drink not only 2 quarts of liquid a day to satisfy normal requirements but also an additional amount to make up for abnormal losses. If daily intake isn't equal to loss, the result is dehydration.

Dehydration reduces the body's blood volume. The blood thickens and circulates sluggishly. Blood vessels in the superficial muscles constrict, reducing circulation to the extremities. This is a natural process that preserves normal blood pressure in the vital core body.

Such impaired circulation has several undesirable results:

• It can affect a person's thinking by failing to provide the brain with sufficient oxygen and other essentials.

• Because dehydration reduces blood flow to the muscles, weakness and fatigue can result.

• In addition, dehydration in hot weather reduces the efficiency of the body's cooling system, contributing directly to heatstroke and heat exhaustion.

• According to Dr. Everett Howard, dehydration almost always is associated with hypothermia and frostbite because impaired circulation in the extremities supersensitizes a person to the effects of cold.

The prevention and cure for dehydration is an adequate intake of liquids. In hot, dry climates, a parched throat will remind you of fluid needs. Drink as much as possible whenever you're thirsty. In cold weather, or when the cause of dehydration is diarrhea, the warning signal of thirst may be absent.

"The problem in cold weather is that you don't get parched as you do in the desert, so you don't feel thirsty," warns Bob Newman, who has climbed major peaks in Alaska, Yukon Territory, Oregon, and Washington. "To avoid dehydration in the mountains, you simply must force yourself to take in as much liquid as possible, much more than you actually feel like drinking."

Newman emphasizes that recognizing the symptoms of dehydration is important in avoiding the problem. He describes his observation of one dehydration case.

"One fellow started stumbling near the summit of Mt. Logan, then fell. We asked him which way camp was, and he pointed the wrong way: straight over a cliff. He was totally disoriented.

"And his urine was so dark it looked like blood. We thought he had a bladder infection. But we put him in a tent and gave him lots of liquids. Within a day he was fine and continued with no more problems. Darkening urine should have warned us of what was happening. Dehydration can develop over a period of days. As it does, the person's urine gradually gets darker."

Dr. Everett Howard relates another experience with dehydration. While climbing 12 hard hours with packs, he and a companion had failed to eat or to drink sufficient liquids. When they reached their goal, they were so tired they simply went to bed.

"Despite our exhaustion, neither of us could sleep. We were restless and kept having strange, weird dreams. At 2 A.M. we were both wide awake, so we boiled a big pot of soup and salted it heavily. We ate cup after cup of it. In no time, we felt refreshed and relaxed, and we slept the rest of the night.

"This was just an example of dehydration and possibly salt depletion. After a hard day a person should always eat and drink before going to bed to replenish salt and liquids lost during the day."

Whenever you're going into the field, make provision for adequate water. In desert country or other hot areas, plan to carry at least a gallon of drinking water a day for every person. If you're backpacking, of course, that's impossible so find out in advance about water sources, making sure that suitable streams or springs are available.

Also remember that natural water sources may be contaminated. In the high mountains, stream water normally is drinkable, but in recent years Giardiasis, which causes violent diarrhea, has become quite common. Unless you can drink directly from springs flowing from underground, you should purify any water. You can kill Giardia by raising water to the boiling point just briefly. In the lowlands, purify all water before drinking. Boil it for 5 minutes at sea level; add 1 minute for each added 1,000 feet of elevation. At 8,000 feet, for example, you'd have to boil the water 13 minutes to sterilize it.

If the water is muddy or has other particles, strain it through a clean cloth. If boiling is impossible, use halazone or iodine tablets, available at sports shops or drug stores, to purify water. However, bacteriologists say these chemicals won't kill Giardia.

As part of a desert survival pack or automobile emergency kit, carry a desert still. The only materials needed are a 6-foot-square of *clear* plastic, a piece of surgical rubber tubing about 4 or 5 feet long, and a can with at least a 1-quart capacity. To make the still, dig a round hole about 3 feet across and 18 inches deep. Set the can at the bottom of the hole, in the middle. Put one end of the tubing into the can so it touches the bottom, and lay the other end outside of the hole. Spread the plastic over the hole and cover the edges with dirt and rock so that it won't slip. It should be air tight. Be sure the top end of the tube is accessible. Place a rock in the middle of the plastic to form a funnel shape with its center directly over the can and only an inch or two above the lip of the can. As the sun beats down on the plastic, air in the hole will get hotter than air outside. Moisture in the warmer air will condense on the underside of the cooler plastic and then run down and drip into the can. To increase production of water, put green leaves or pulpy cacti in the hole. After enough water accumulates, you suck it from the can through the tubing.

Part of your hot-weather survival equipment should be the materials for a desert still. Practice at home before your life depends on it.

In winter, water can be as scarce as it is in the desert. Carry a water bottle, drink from it often, and refill it at every chance. Use water-purification tablets.

A stove is especially helpful to winter campers for melting snow to provide water. Beware of gasoline on your skin; it can cause instant frostbite.

In conditions that can cause hypothermia, drink hot liquids to help maintain body heat. Sit on a pad to prevent snow from draining heat away.

Finding water in winter can be a problem because most water sources are frozen. So carry a quart of drinking water. Refill the water bottle at every stream or place where snow is melting. If no open water is available, refill the bottle with snow after you take a drink. Water in the bottle will melt the snow although you may have to keep the bottle close to your body to prevent its freezing.

Perhaps the most important items to carry in winter are a small gasoline or Sterno stove and metal cup or pot for melting snow or ice for drinking water. Most experienced winter campers agree that a stove and pot are critical winter items.

Fatigue

Fatigue is a common problem that in itself doesn't threaten survival but can contribute to problems that do. One cause of fatigue is an inadequate supply of body fuel. Sugar, derived from the food you eat, is the body's energy source. Sugar in the bloodstream plays approximately the same part that gasoline does in a car engine. When your body's fuel supply is restricted or depleted, your body runs poorly.

Waste products, primarily lactic acid and carbon dioxide in the muscles, also cause fatigue. Wastes form during exercise. If exercise is moderate or is interspersed with rest, oxygen in the bloodstream cleanses wastes from the muscles. During prolonged exertion, wastes may build up faster than oxygen in the blood can get rid of them. The result is fatigue.

Fatigue can lead to injury. Fatigue impairs strength and coordination, making you vulnerable to cuts, sprains, or broken bones from stumbling or falling.

Fatigue also contributes to exposure problems. In producing heat, the body is, again, much like a car engine. Just as gasoline burning in the cylinders of an engine produces heat, so does combustion of food in the body. Friction in the engine creates additional heat as pistons slide along cylinder walls and rods whirr within bearings. In the body, the "friction" of muscular activity does the same. In fact, only 20 to 30 percent of energy burned during exercise goes into motion. The rest is converted into heat. The harder you work, the more heat your muscles produce.

In the car engine, heat produced by combustion and friction is largely wasted. But in the human body, heat is essential for warmth in cold weather. Fatigue undermines this vital source of heat by making muscles sluggish and inefficient. They're not able to produce enough heat to keep a person warm under bitter conditions. Fatigue sets you up for hypothermia and frostbite.

Fatigue also may affect your judgment. The brain is a delicate, sensitive organ. It needs a constantly rich energy supply. When fatigue depletes energy reserves, the brain is affected. If you're ever walking a thin line of survival, poor judgment could be fatal.

Under mild conditions, fatigue may seem insignificant. But when conditions are severe, preventing fatigue could be one step toward survival.

One form of prevention is to regulate physical activity. Here again, the analogy of the car engine is applicable. Stop-and-go city driving is notorious for wasting fuel and fouling engines. Stop-and-go hiking, where you push yourself at full speed and then are forced to stop for rest, has a similar effect. Your body burns fuel inefficiently, and waste products build up in your muscles.

Sporadic exertion accelerates fatigue in other ways. While pushing yourself hard, you pant. Your breathing muscles must work harder than normal. And while you pant, you gulp in large quantities of cold air that must be warmed in the lungs, wasting additional energy. In addition, as you labor your muscles produce excessive heat. This heat can't be stored for later use, so most of it is radiated away. It's wasted. And worse, the heavy exertion may make you sweat. Now when you stop, you chill, and your body must burn more fuel just to keep you warm. Thus, sporadic, stop-and-go exertion starts a fatiguing chain of events that can be broken only by regulation of physical activity.

The best approach is to set a steady, easily sustained pace. Each individual should find his own natural pace. A couple of guidelines may help. If you're getting breathless, you're probably moving too fast. Try to move at a rate at which you can carry on a conversation. Also, avoid sweating heavily. If you've allowed for good ventilation and still get soaked with sweat, you may be pushing too hard.

A good way to conserve energy is to *stay* warm. When you stop, put on clothing to preserve heat produced during exercise. *Rewarming, once you've chilled, takes a lot more energy than staying warm.*

On any outing, get plenty of rest. Muscles need recovery periods. On the trail, stop for 10 minutes every hour. At night, use a good sleeping bag and a foam pad under it to insure sound sleep. When I was a kid, I had a cheap bag. In any weather below 50° F., I'd practically freeze at night. By the end of a 3-day hike, I'd be so fatigued from lack of sleep that I could hardly think or walk. Good sleep is important in survival.

A good diet is also important. In the overall scheme of survival, food doesn't rank in importance with shelter and water. Without shelter and water, a person may die within 2 or 3 days. Without food, he may live several weeks. But especially under cold or exhausting conditions, adequate diet is significant in maintaining energy, warmth, and strength. Long-range menu planning is beyond the scope of this book, but a basic understanding of food will help you plan sufficient meals.

Energy is measured in calories. Some foods are better suited to supply calories than others. Food is classified by groups—fats, proteins, and carbohydrates. Major sources of fats are fatty meat, butter and margarine, cheese, egg yolks, and nuts. For a given amount of food weight, fats offer over twice as many calories as the two other food groups.

Sources of protein are lean meat, milk, cheese, and eggs; cereals such as wheat and oats; and legumes such as peas and beans. Proteins supply basic body-building materials not found in the other groups, so any diet should include protein. However, proteins are hard to digest, so a protein-rich diet isn't the best for outdoors activity.

Carbohydrates, the sugars and starches, offer only as many calories as protein, but carbohydrates digest much more quickly and easily. Carbohydrates can go from the stomach to the bloodstream in a couple of hours or less. Because carbohydrates digest easily, they should provide the bulk of calories in an outdoor diet. According to internist Dr. Ken Magee, carbohydrates should provide 60 to 70 percent of an outdoor person's total caloric intake.

Carbohydrates are classified as either simple or complex. According to Magee, simple carbohydrates are available from the pure sugars found in candy, pastries, and other sweets. Complex carbohydrates are available from fruits, vegetables, and starchy foods.

Magee stresses that a person's diet should include plenty of complex carbohydrates as well as simple carbohydrates. The problem with eating only simple carbohydrates is that the blood-sugar level, because sugar from simple carbohydrates can reach the bloodstream in an hour or less, rises rapidly after eating. Not long after the rise, the blood-sugar level may drop off abruptly, giving a person the feeling of fatigue.

Complex carbohydrates, on the other hand, take longer to reach the bloodstream—up to three or four hours or more. The addition of these slower-digesting carbohydrates to an outdoor diet insures that a high level of energy will be spread over an extended period of time, eliminating the extreme ups and downs experienced when only simple carbohydrates are eaten.

In the outdoors, don't eat three big meals daily. Instead, eat small meals frequently. A full stomach competes with skeletal muscles for the use of circulating blood. If you eat a huge meal and then hit the trail, your circulatory system can't adequately serve both the stomach and the working muscles at once. A stomach ache is a likely outcome. Besides, a heavy meal of fats and proteins offers little immediate energy. The energy from these foods may take up to 10 hours to reach your bloodstream.

Start the day with a light breakfast of cereal. Then throughout the day eat small portions of carbohydrate-rich foods such as gorp (a mixture of raisins, peanuts, and

Eat snacks of carbohydrate-rich foods throughout the day to maintain a high level of energy in cold weather. This hiker carries gorp in a plastic bottle.

chocolate), candy bars, or sandwiches made with jelly or honey. Then at night have your big meal. A dinner rich in fats and proteins will digest overnight and give you energy the next day.

You can plan a menu by estimating your daily caloric needs. At rest a person burns about 1100 calories per day for each 100 pounds of body weight. A 180-pound man, then, requires about 2000 calories to meet basic metabolic requirements; a 120-pound woman needs about 1300. During work, these requirements rise drastically. The amount depends on physical conditioning, the type of activity, steepness of hills being climbed, the weight of load, and other things. But a reasonable estimate of energy expenditure for 8 hours of hard hiking would be 4500 calories for the 180-pound man, 3000 for the 120-pound woman.

If you're camping by car or boat, getting sufficient calories is no problem. You can take along as much food as you want. But if you're backpacking, menu planning probably will require more thought. Choose foods carefully to provide the needed energy. Books on nutrition, available at libraries, have charts showing the number of calories contained in certain foods. You can get the same information from county extension agencies or U.S. Department of Agriculture offices.

Regardless of the kind of outing you're taking, plan for emergencies. Take food enough for several extra days.

6
CLOTHING

Adequate clothing is essential for keeping the body warm. Cold-weather clothing works by trapping a layer of dead air next to the skin. This dead air holds radiated body heat, thereby forming a shell of warm air around the body. Some materials, because of their structure and bulk, can trap more air than others. The more air that clothing can trap, the warmer it is.

Staying warm, however, isn't simply a matter of wearing the warmest clothing available. Because the air temperature, climatic conditions, and levels of physical activity can vary greatly on any outing, clothing must be chosen not just for greatest warmth but also for heat-regulating qualities.

Clothing Materials

Wool is the best all-around cold-weather material. For one thing, wool has good bulk, so it is warm in relation to its weight. Equally important, it wicks moisture away from the skin to reduce heat loss through conduction.

Perhaps the most unusual attribute of wool is that it insulates even when wet. I found out the value of this property on one outing. Rain started falling my first day in the mountains and continued steadily for 8 days. My heavy wool pants and shirt were soaked from the first day on. But despite near-freezing temperatures and gusty wind, the wool kept me warm and comfortable, something most other clothing materials would have failed to do.

Wool is the best all-around clothing material in cold weather. Author's wife Laura, wearing wool pants and two wool sweaters, is ideally dressed for prevailing weather.

What about down-filled clothing? For its weight, down is the warmest material available. Down garments are ideal for mountain climbing and other activities in extreme low temperatures. Down is also excellent for sedentary outdoorsmen such as ice fishermen or hunters on stand. And it's great for slipping on at rest stops or around camp.

But down has its drawbacks. One is that it's too warm for active outdoors use. Down's incomparable insulation allows little excess body heat to escape. So in any but the coldest temperatures, an active person will overheat and sweat heavily. In addition, down is worthless when wet. It soaks up moisture and gets as soggy as a wet sponge.

In wet conditions, garments filled with synthetic fiber may be better. Many new fibers have been developed. Two, for example, are Hollofil and PolarGuard. Garments and sleeping bags made of these can be bought at most sports shops. For the same degree of warmth, synthetics are slightly heavier than down, but they maintain loft (bulk) and warmth when wet.

One poor cold-weather material is cotton, especially in underwear and socks. Cotton absorbs moisture but has no wicking action. Rather, it holds moisture directly against the skin. This moisture then conducts away body heat, causing rapid chilling. A sweaty T-shirt or cotton socks will stay clammy for hours, refrigerating the body.

In place of cotton, wear underclothes with wool content. Or wear fishnet underwear. Some brands of fishnet are 100 percent cotton themselves, but because of their structure, they wick moisture from the skin and have dead-air spaces to reduce conduction. Wear wool or nylon socks in place of cotton.

Probably the poorest cold-weather material of all is denim. Denim jeans provide practically no insulation, and when they're wet they provide about as much warmth and flexibility as sheet steel.

The Layer System

The secret to regulating body heat for maximum warmth is to dress in layers. Four thin garments may offer the same degree of warmth as one thick garment, but the four layers allow much greater flexibility. That's because the layers can be shed or added as temperature, wind, exertion, and other variables dictate.

Over wool or fishnet underwear, wear several light-to-medium-weight wool garments. The number of layers will depend on climate and season. They should be comfortably loose rather than tight. An early-fall combination might include a lightweight wool shirt for general active wear and a heavier one for evenings and cooler days. In winter, you might need three or four wool shirts or sweaters. I personally prefer shirts because they're more convenient to take off and put on than slipover sweaters. Also, shirts can be unbuttoned or buttoned, depending on the level of activity, for better heat regulation.

Fishnet underwear provides dead air spaces to retain body heat. By unbuttoning shirt under certain conditions, author regulates body heat to avoid sweating.

For camp wear and other inactive periods, a down or synthetic-fiber vest or jacket rounds out a good clothing system. These extra-warm garments are ideal for periods when you're not generating excess heat through exercise.

On your legs, wear wool underwear bottoms and wool pants over them. Some hikers prefer knickers with long wool socks because they allow better leg movement and heat regulation than long pants. Mountain climber Bob Newman points out that knicker socks can be rolled down inside gaiters and wind pants to allow ventilation for the legs.

The body's greatest heat loss occurs through the head and neck. Fifty percent or more of heat radiated from the body is radiated from this area, so adequate protection here is vital. Under moderate conditions, any comfortable hat with ear flaps might do as head protection. But for cold weather with wind and moisture, a wool sock hat is hard to beat. It's especially good in combination with a long wool scarf. The neck is vulnerable to rapid cooling, so I find that nothing contributes more to overall warmth than a scarf. Using a sock hat and scarf together, you can roll the hat up or down and wrap your neck in the scarf or remove the scarf altogether, giving good versatility in regulating body heat.

A great deal of body heat is radiated from head and neck if they're unprotected on a cold day. Balaclava shown here gives high degree of protection.

In cold weather, don't handle metal objects with bare hands. Metal drains away body heat. Remember that mittens are warmer than gloves.

An alternative is the balaclava, a heavy sock hat that rolls down to cover the entire face and neck except for the eyes and nose. Balaclavas are good in severe conditions where the face may need protection to prevent frostbite.

Heat drains through your head as you sleep. If you're getting cold at night, pull a sock hat over your head. Prevention of heat loss here will help keep your body warm.

Hands and feet are areas of major heat loss, so they deserve special attention. If dexterity isn't essential, mittens are better than gloves. Mittens reduce the surface area exposed to wind and cold. In extreme cold, wear an inner wool mitten and an outer nylon wind mitt. In moderate weather, wool gloves are good. Cotton and leather gloves or mittens are poor for the same reasons that cotton clothing is.

Next to your feet wear thin, snug-fitting socks of nylon or smooth-finished wool. Over these wear heavy wool socks. The thin socks wick moisture from the feet, and the thick outer socks provide bulk for warmth. This system also helps prevent blisters. Blisters are caused by slippage between the socks and feet. With snug inner socks and loose-fitting outer socks this slippage takes place between the sock layers rather than against the feet.

Don't wear too many socks. Good circulation is essential to warm feet. One pair of heavy socks in loose-fitting boots will be warmer than two or three pairs if the added socks make your boots fit tight.

The Outer Shell

For insulative clothing to be effective, it must be dry and protected from wind. Wool, particularly, offers little wind resistance, so a windbreaker of some kind adds to its efficiency. Under moderate conditions, a light nylon outer shell is adequate. Where wind and cold may be harsh, a hooded jacket, called an anorak, is better. Anoraks are made of a nylon-cotton blend. The material is not waterproof. It allows moisture from your body to pass through, but it's tight enough to cut the wind and to shed some moisture.

In heavy rain or wet snow, a waterproof shell is needed. Some waterproof garments are made of rubber-coated nylon, others of rubberized canvas. The rubber-coated nylon garments are lightweight and rugged, so they're good for backcountry use. Rubberized-canvas raingear is heavier but can stand a lot of punishment, so it's good for boating, snowmobiling, and other sports where weight is no problem. Cheap plastic raingear may be all right for emergency summer use, but it's fragile. Where prolonged bad weather is likely, don't stake your comfort or life on such flimsy equipment.

A waterproof parka should have a hood, or you should have waterproof headgear. If your body needs protection, your head needs it all the more. A rainsuit should include pants.

Some hikers like a poncho, especially for backpacking since it can be worn over the pack. Another choice is the cagoule—a long, waterproof anorak. It hangs below the knees and is good for emergency bivouacs. You can sit down and pull your legs inside the cagoule for full-length protection. If you can't find these garments at general outdoors stores, try shops or mail-order houses that specialize in backpacking and mountaineering equipment.

For most trips, you'll probably want to choose either a windproof or waterproof shell rather than carry both. In high country where wind and cold are severe, a wind-breaker is the obvious choice. In country where you expect rain or wet snow, probably you'll go with a waterproof outer shell. Raingear, however, makes a poor all-around shell, especially during prolonged activity. The waterproof material doesn't breathe, so moisture from your body condenses on the inside, forming a water layer that will soak your clothing.

A relatively new material called Gore-Tex eliminates most condensation problems while giving protection against rain and snow. If Gore-Tex garments are made properly they're fully waterproof, yet they breathe so that moisture doesn't condense on the inside to get you wet. Gore-Tex parka and pants can serve as an all-around outer shell under any conditions.

Footgear

Feet may be your only means of transportation and your lifeline to safety, so choice of footgear deserves careful thought. Buy the best boots you can afford, and get boots suited to the worst terrain and climatic conditions you'll encounter.

Some hikers and backpackers advocate wearing tennis shoes. For trail hiking in summer, tennis shoes have a place. But for winter hiking they're out, and for backpacking or off-trail outings at any time, I think they're a poor choice. The potential for jamming feet between logs or banging them on rocks is too great.

Leather boots provide considerably more support and protection than canvas shoes. For general hiking, any comfortable leather boots are fine. Those with soft crepe-rubber soles are good in rocky country because rocks bite into the soft soles for good traction.

For carrying heavy loads and walking on steep, bare slopes, lug soles such as Vibram are better. They insure good traction, and the heavy, stiff soles give support and protection for the feet against twisting and bruising.

Mountaineering boots with lug soles are popular with climbers and backpackers. These boots are noninsulated and nonwaterproof, so they breathe well. But wool socks must be worn for warmth, and the boots must be treated with oil or wax preparations for water repellency.

My personal choice for hiking and backpacking is insulated leather boots with 8-inch tops. These are made

Three of the author's favorite boot styles. At left are insulated, nonwaterproof leather boots with heavy lug soles; in the center are insulated, waterproof leather boots; and at right are rubber-bottomed, leather-topped boots with thick felt liners. First two types are good for general outdoor use in hot and cold weather. Third type are fine in snow and any cold weather.

in both waterproof or nonwaterproof styles. Both are good for year-around use, but don't rely on the insulation to keep your feet warm in winter. Heavy wool socks are needed. The nonwaterproof boots must be treated for water repellency. I've worn these in deep snow for hours in comfort as long as the temperature was low enough to keep the snow from melting. I've also used the waterproof styles and think they're great, especially in rain, wet snow, or boggy country.

Insulated rubber boots are good for cold, wet weather if you plan to remain in one small area, but they're not made for hiking. If you hike in them, moisture condenses on the inside. Then your socks get wet and you get cold feet.

Shoe-pacs insulated with felt liners are better for winter hiking. These have rubber lowers for protection against moisture and leather uppers for ventilation to prevent condensation inside. Even on snow, these boots will keep your feet warm for days. They're bulky and flexible, so they're unsuited to climbing or skiing. But for snowshoe-ing or moderate winter hiking, they're very good.

Getting the Most from Clothing

Unless you utilize its advantages, even the best clothing is worthless. First, put layers to work to regulate body heat. When you're exerting yourself, unbutton or take off your heavy shirt to allow ventilation, and take off your scarf and sock hat so excess heat can escape from your head. Do this before you overheat and start sweating. Sweaty clothing will chill you quickly.

When you stop to rest or you arrive at camp, put on your heavy shirt or down coat and hat and scarf as soon as the danger of sweating is past. Preserve the warmth you've generated through exercise. Finally, don't wait until you're soaked from rain or chilled by wind to put on your outer shell. Put it on before any damage is done.

7
SHELTER

A person exposed to severe heat, cold, or precipitation can't live long. He must have shelter. Hot-weather shelter must provide shade to keep you cool. Cold-weather shelter must protect you from wind, rain, and snow to keep you warm. The fundamentals for building each are, however, essentially the same.

Tents

Under most conditions, the most reliable shelter is a tent. A tent can't be classified as emergency shelter, but a good tent can avert many emergencies. Bruce Wadlington at Crater Lake National Park says many winter campers fail to carry tents on ski tours and often find themselves in trouble as a result. He believes all campers who've had little winter shelter-building experience should rely on a tent.

This also holds true for other seasonal camping. On a long backpacking trip one September I decided not to take a tent, expecting to use natural shelter if an emergency arose. I ended up spending 8 days in pouring rain under a makeshift lean-to. The experience was bad, and it taught me the value of dependable shelter. Now I carry a tent for primary shelter and never have regretted it.

Heavy-canvas wall tents and umbrella tents provide excellent protection, but transporting them is a big chore. For backpacking, a lightweight nylon tent is needed. This tent must have two layers of protection. Single-wall waterproof tents are acceptable for summer emergencies, but in other seasons (when prolonged bad weather may engulf you), a waterproof tent is next to worthless. It doesn't breathe, so water vapor from your body condenses on the inside of the walls. Your sleeping bag and

Nylon tent should have two layers. The nonwaterproof inner layer allows moisture to escape from inside. The waterproof outer layer keeps out precipitation.

clothing mop up this moisture. Within 2 or 3 days, your sleeping bag will be soaked through. A double-layer tent solves this problem. The nonwaterproof inner wall allows water vapor from inside to pass through. A waterproof fly (or tarp, as some people call it) put up over the tent keeps out rain and snow.

Emergency Shelter

Your owning a suitable tent doesn't mean you'll never face the need for emergency shelter. Nobody carries a tent everywhere. I've got caught away from camp at night several times and have had to improvise shelter.

Observe a few principles in planning shelter. In cold weather, your best bet usually is to place the entrance crosswind. If it's straight downwind, smoke from your fire will eddy into your face and snow will drift over the entrance. Wind blowing across the entrance will carry smoke and snow away.

In hot weather, if the wind isn't too strong, you may want the entrance facing toward the wind so it will blow into the shelter to cool you.

Cold ground or snow rapidly conducts heat from your body. In cold weather, always insulate yourself from the ground with a layer of clothing or tree boughs.

In planning a shelter site, beware of natural dangers. Don't build where rocks or dead branches will fall on you, or where an avalanche may sweep down. And during snowstorms, stay away from leeward slopes where snow will drift heavily and where a cornice may develop above you.

Finally, allow time to plan a shelter. If you can see you'll have to stay out overnight, don't push yourself until you're too exhausted to do the job. Make shelter before darkness overtakes you. Of particular importance, seek shelter before damage is done, before you're soaking wet, or before the hot sun starts to raise your body temperature.

From the beginning, plan emergency shelter equal to the conditions so you don't have to rebuild it or find better shelter as things get worse. But don't waste valuable energy building a palace. The best emergency shelter is the simplest one that will meet your needs. First, try to use natural protection. One winter, two friends and I got

Natural shelter such as this cliff is a substantial help during a short or long stop. It offers protection from wind, reflects heat, and makes a fire more effective.

caught in a downpour. The sopping brush offered little comfort, but we found a huge overhanging cliff. It gave protection throughout the night better than anything we could have built.

A cave can be ideal. Or you may be able to crawl under a windfall that has dense branches or into the depression left by the roots of a blown-over tree. A dense spruce or fir thicket often offers ideal shelter from wind and rain. In the desert, rimrocks or high sage may give adequate protection from sun or heavy wind.

When natural shelter isn't available, construct your own. It's easy if you're prepared. As discussed in Chapter 15, you should have twine or cord with you, and you should have some kind of covering. I like to carry a 9' × 12' plastic tarp. Tarps of 1-mil plastic are compact and lightweight, and they are inexpensive. They do tear easily, so a tarp may be good for only one or two shelters. In hot country where shade is needed, a Space Blanket is good. Its shiny side reflects the sun's heat.

These coverings can be used over any framework. Two good ones are the A-frame and lean-to. The A-frame is quicker. In emergencies, I've thrown up A-frames in a matter of minutes. The easiest way is to lash a ridgepole 6 to 10 feet long to the trunk of a tree. Even simpler is to lay a ridgepole in a low tree crotch, if you can find such a convenience.

If a support tree isn't handy, cut two poles 6 to 7 feet long. Use a shear lashing (see illustration) to bind the poles near the top, then move the poles to form an X. Set the ridgepole across the top of the X. Then drape the tarp over the frame and anchor it to the ground with logs or rocks. You should have shelter within 15 minutes.

To make a lean-to, lash a pole between two trees, or tie cord or twine tightly between the trees. Tie your tarp over this ridgepole, and anchor it to the ground in back at about a 45° angle. If the wind is blowing or snow is falling hard enough to build up on the plastic, additional support

From the 9' x 12' plastic tarp he carries in his survival pack, plus three poles, author put together this A-frame emergency shelter in 10 minutes and spent a reasonably comfortable night during a heavy rainstorm.

In making an A-frame shelter, use a shear lashing to join the two "doorway" poles. Lay poles side by side and wrap cord snugly around them several times. Then wrap cord ends between poles and around initial wrappings. Tie ends together. Practice at home using handles of garden tools. When poles are spread to form "A," lashing tightens.

Plastic tarp in survival kit can also be used to cover a lean-to frame. Crossbars help plastic to withstand wind and fairly heavy snow.

Face entrance of emergency lean-to cross-wind so that smoke will drift past. Platform of logs prevents fire from melting down into snow. Don't sit on snow or cold ground. Put down a pad or boughs.

is needed. Lay two side-support poles angling 45° from the ridgepole to the ground. Tie a couple of cross poles, parallel with the ridgepole, from one side pole to the other. Anchor the tarp over this frame.

A lean-to can be made without a frame. A large log will substitute as a ridgepole. In desert country, you might use brush to support the front of the tarp, or you might stack rocks. If you're boating or canoeing, tip your craft on its side, support it with paddles or oars, and use the side of the craft as a ridgepole.

If for some reason you get caught without the plastic, you can roof any A-frame or lean-to with natural materials such as slabs of bark or boughs. Frequently you can pull big chunks of bark off rotted logs. Evergreen boughs make a good thatching although they require some work. Cut boughs with forks near the butts, and slip these forks over cross poles on the shelter frame. Add several overlapping layers until the roof is thick enough to shed rain or to support falling snow. Keep in mind that the cutting of live branches is a procedure that should be resorted to only in an emergency.

Build your shelter large enough so you can stretch out to be comfortable and high enough to sit up in, but don't make it any larger than necessary. A small shelter will be warmer than a large one. For greatest warmth, build a fire near the entrance, where you can get its direct heat and heat reflected off the ceiling. A body-length fire parallel to the entrance will keep you warm from head to foot.

Another quick shelter that might be more appropriate at times is an "umbrella." Tie the tarp in the center over an upright pole, which might be a de-limbed sapling, walking stick, or camera tripod. Tie the tarp's four corners out and stake them down.

Unless your tarp has grommets, tying cord to the plastic can be hard. To solve this problem, wrap a limb stub or a rock in the corner of the plastic, tie your cord just above this, and snug the cord against the rock or stub.

Snow Shelter

The shelters already mentioned will work in most situations. But on deep snow in bitter weather, a trench may be better. In some snow you may be able to stamp out a trench, but usually some digging will be required. The trench should be deep enough and long enough so you can sit up and lie down. It should also be covered to keep out falling snow and to hold in your body heat. Use your pack, snowshoes, skis, and other gear as covering or support for covering. If possible, cut snow blocks for a roof, or use dense boughs.

Again, don't lie directly on the snow. Put down a bed of boughs or sit on some clothing or a pack.

To simplify trench digging, look for natural depressions such as tree wells under the dense branches of fir and spruce trees. You may have to dig very little. Don't place your trench at the bottom of a draw. Cold air sinks. Pick a site up the hill where air temperature will be slightly warmer.

If you're planning long winter outings, particularly above timberline, you may want to learn how to dig a snow cave or build an igloo. These hardly can be classed as emergency shelters. They're planned undertakings, often used by experienced campers as substitutes for tents. Most books on mountaineering and advanced survival give details for making snow caves and igloos.

8
FIRE

Not only your comfort but also your life could depend on your ability to build a fire under seemingly impossible conditions.

Veteran outdoorsman Doug Kittredge got caught out in heavy rain one fall. He was soaking wet. Overcome by fatigue, he couldn't reach camp, so he stopped to build a fire. All the wood was saturated with water. Kittredge was shivering so badly he could scarcely hold a match. But because he was experienced, he got the fire going and had a reasonably comfortable night. Looking back, Kittredge realizes he was suffering the initial symptoms of hypothermia. If he'd failed to light that fire, he might have died.

Fire is invaluable for several reasons. In Kittredge's case, warmth is most obvious. Just as important, he was able to dry his clothing. Dry clothes are not only more comfortable but also are much warmer than wet ones.

Fire can do more than provide warmth. You can cook a meal or boil water over a fire. You can use a fire to signal for help. Fire also provides light, a necessity not only for working at night but also for psychological well-being. The cavelike darkness of deep woods can be oppressive. A dancing orange flame dispels the uneasiness of darkness and loneliness.

Finally, fire means home. The feeling of being lost can cause panic. When panic strikes, disaster is close at hand. The cure? Build a fire. Where your fire is, camp is also. You no longer feel lost and can evaluate your situation with a clear mind.

Fire Starters

The key to a guaranteed fire is preparation. Don't wait until you're wet, freezing, and lost to think about building a fire. The time to think about it is now.

First, you need a fire starter. By "fire starter" I mean the initial source of flame. A book of paper matches stuck in your shirt pocket won't do. For general fire starting, large wooden matches are good. You can dip these in melted paraffin to moisture-proof them. Carry the matches in a watertight container. The soft, white plastic bottles with screw-on lids are good because they won't crack. Tear a striker from a match box and glue it in the lid. A cigarette lighter with a visible supply of liquid butane is also a handy, general-purpose fire starter.

These fire starters aren't guaranteed. Despite all precautions, the matches can still get wet, and the lighter can malfunction. Always have a backup starter for emergencies. One good choice is commercially made waterproof matches. For example, Coghlan's Windproof and Waterproof Matches can be soaked in water for several hours and will still light, and they're impossible to blow out. The sparklerlike flame lasts about 5 seconds, plenty of time to get a fire going.

Perhaps an even more reliable emergency fire starter is flint-and-steel. One modern version, the Metal Match, is

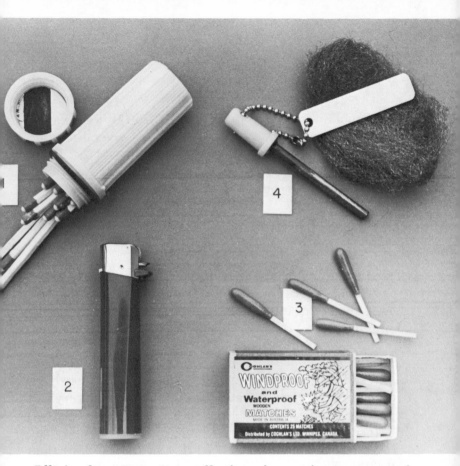

Effective fire starters: 1) paraffined wooden matches in waterproof container (note striker glued inside lid), 2) cigarette lighter (type with visible butane supply is best), 3) commercially made windproof and waterproof matches, and 4) Metal Match (a modern version of flint and steel) plus steel wool for catching the spark.

sold in sporting-goods shops. With a Metal Match, sparks are produced by scraping a flat steel striker along a flint rod. A "spark catcher" is needed to turn these sparks into flame. The best I've found is steel wool in either 00 or 000 grade. Even if it's soaking wet, steel wool will light. Just shake the water out of it first. Scrape a spark from the Metal Match onto the wool, and then blow on it. Steel wool doesn't produce a flame, but it turns into a mass of red-hot filaments that will ignite tinder.

Tinder

Often a fire starter alone isn't adequate. In wet weather when wood is damp, a starter must burn several minutes in order to dry the wood enough to set it ablaze. That's when tinder is needed. Under wet conditions, you can't rely on your surroundings to provide tinder, so carry some with you.

By my definition, tinder is any material that serves as a link between fire starter and firewood. A good tinder must have several qualities:

• It must light easily in cold and damp weather.
• It must be reasonably windproof and moisture proof.
• It must burn long enough, say 5 minutes, to dry soggy kindling.

Three good tinders are:

• Sterno.

Sterno, or canned heat, is a jellylike substance used, for instance, in fondue cooking. You can get it at grocery and sporting-goods stores.

Sterno rates an "A" for resistance to wind and moisture. To start a fire with Sterno, light it in the can and then stack kindling over it. Once the fire is going, fish out the Sterno (use a stick) for later use. A small can of Sterno burns for about 40 minutes. Figuring it takes 5 minutes to start a fire, you can build eight fires with one can.

• Sawdust saturated with paint thinner.

Paint-thinner-saturated sawdust burns well in wind and will burn if damp, but a good soaking will put it out. Carry sawdust in a watertight plastic bottle. A bottle about 3 inches high and 1½ inches in diameter holds enough to start four or five fires.

• Hexamine tablets.

You can get Hexamine tablets, made to heat Army field rations, at surplus stores. These tablets are fairly wind resistant but are hard to light if wet. One tube contains six tablets, enough to start at least three fires.

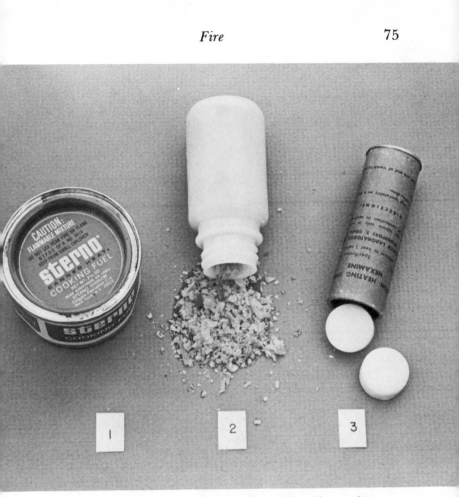

Here are three effective tinders you can carry: 1) small can of Sterno, 2) sawdust saturated with paint thinner and kept in a watertight plastic bottle, and 3) Hexamine tablets (designed to heat army field rations).

You can light any of these tinders with a match, of course, but flint-and-steel will work also. If you're using Sterno, simply strike a spark into the can. In weather below freezing, this technique may not work. So lay a small piece of steel wool on the Sterno, strike a spark on it, then blow hard. As the steel wool gets red hot, the Sterno will take right off. Paint-thinner-soaked sawdust and Hexamine tablets can be lit the same way.

Sawdust saturated with pain
thinner will burn well i
wind and will burn even
slightly damp. But a goo
soaking with water will put
out.

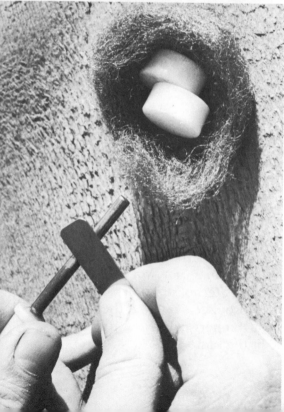

One effective way to light
Hexamine tablets is to strike a
spark into steel wool and then
blow on it till the tinder takes
off. Hexamine tablets have
good wind resistance but are
hard to light if damp.

Your survival pack should contain fire-starting materials. I carry a lighter or wooden matches for general fire building. For emergencies, I have a backup kit containing waterproof matches or a Metal Match (a form of flint and steel) and pad of steel wool, and one of the tinders I've just been discussing. I keep these sealed in a plastic bag and don't use them until they're absolutely needed.

Survival pack should have a plastic bag containing fire-starting materials for emergencies. Contents of this kit are: 1) paraffined matches in waterproof container, 2) Metal Match, 3) steel wool, and 4) small can of Sterno. Kit should be used for emergencies only, not for routine fire building.

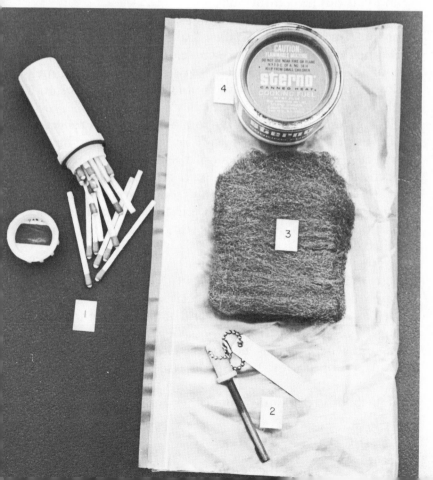

How to Build a Fire

Most fire-starting failures, I believe, result from poor preparation, usually brought on by a feeling of urgency. A person in a hurry strikes a match before assembling the necessary ingredients. To guarantee yourself a fire, prepare thoroughly.

First, select a good site. Look for a spot protected from wind and rain or snow on the leeward side of a cliff, rock, log, or big tree. Don't build your fire under a branch loaded with snow that could crash down on it. In other words, take time to select a site where the fire will survive and you can be comfortable.

Even if you're in a hurry, think safety. Never build a fire on pine or fir needles, fallen leaves, or scattered limbs. Scrape clear at least a 3-foot circle down to mineral soil so your fire won't get away. On snow or ice, a fire will melt downward. To prevent this problem, build the fire on a platform of logs or large branches.

To get maximum warmth from a fire, make a reflector. If your fire is next to a cliff or big log, you have a reflector. If not, build a wall of rocks around three sides of the fire. Don't make a complete circle. That just blocks heat from you. If you can't find rocks, prop a couple of short poles up nearly vertically and then stack other poles on top of each against the vertical poles to form a reflector.

The final step in preparation is gathering firewood. Start small. You can't build a fire with branches the size of baseball bats. For kindling, collect twigs no thicker than matchsticks, or get thin chips and splinters. Gather kindling from standing trees if possible, rather than off the ground where it may be soggy. Look under the heavy branches of evergreens. Spruce trees, especially, often have a wealth of dead twigs along the trunk under an umbella of green limbs. Pine cones and pine needles are good. Also, look for punky logs or stumps from which to tear dry wood.

Most important, get plenty of kindling wood. A handful won't do. The kindling must be dense enough for flame to reach from one twig to the next, and it must burn long enough to dry and ignite larger firewood. Get enough kindling to burn 10 minutes or more. Collecting an adequate kindling supply is a vital step in fire building.

In addition, gather a stack of branches ½ inch to 1 inch in diameter. Then stockpile some bigger pieces. The significant idea is to have a gradation from small to large and to have an ample supply so the initial blaze won't go out while you're frantically searching for more wood. Much less time will be wasted by preparing first than trying to start the fire prematurely and failing.

Often a source of fine kindling are the dead lower branches of standing conifers such as spruce and pine. Start with twigs about as thin as matchsticks.

Have everything ready before you try to ignite a fire. Then put down your tinder and pile your kindling over it. A gradation of bigger material should be prepared and within easy reach.

Your stockpile enables you to tend the fire closely, adding larger pieces, instead of looking around frantically for more fuel.

When you're confident one match will do the job, put your tinder down and pile kindling over it in pyramid fashion. Then add a number of medium-size branches. Light the tinder on the upwind side so the flame will creep into the fuel supply. As the fire grows, keep adding wood to build a good base of hot coals.

If you've carried with you a reliable fire starter and tinder and you've made a thorough field preparation, you'll have a comfortable blaze going in minutes.

That's not the end of fire building, however. One step remains, and that's putting it out after it has served its purpose. Never leave a fire burning. Ideally, you should build your fire near a creek or spring so you can douse it. If that's not possible, stir mineral soil into the coals until you can lay your hand on them without jerking it away. Pack dirt over the fire bed until you see no hint of smoke. Then your fire will be safe to leave.

9

TO FIND YOUR WAY

If you've read the story of Hansel and Gretel, you'll recall that Hansel dropped white pebbles as he traveled. He and Gretel easily found their way home by following this trail of pebbles. But the second time, unable to get pebbles, Hansel marked the trail with bread crumbs. He had the right idea, but it backfired. Birds ate all the crumbs. Hansel and Gretel ended up lost.

Getting lost is not uncommon. In fact, most search-and-rescue missions are to look for lost people. That's because many outdoorsmen, like Hansel and Gretel, rely on something like breadcrumbs rather than something solid like pebbles to guide them. They go into the field unprepared, with no reliable means of finding their way.

Most country offers plenty of "pebbles" to follow—peaks or ridges, streams and drainages, meadows, clear-cuts, roads, and trails. Following these is mainly a matter of learning to observe. As you travel, note and memorize landmarks and your relation to them. Look in all directions. In particular, turn around often to see the same perspective you'll have on the return trip.

Be aware of time and distance as well. Check your watch to see how long you've traveled one way, and allow time for the return. Record mentally how many drainages you've crossed or peaks you've passed. Be conscious of the relation of your travel to the sun's position throughout the day.

Observation of God's pebbles left along the trail is important, but often it isn't enough. Fog or blizzard may obscure landmarks. In flat dense country, you may be unable to see guiding features. In some areas, various peaks and canyons can seem confusingly similar. In such situations, especially if the country is new to you, additional navigation aids are essential. These aids are maps and a compass.

Maps

Recently I met two hikers on the trail.

"How far is it to Grass Lake?" one of them asked me.

"He can't be serious," I thought. "Grass Lake is 40 miles to the north in a different wilderness area."

But he was serious. The two had no idea where they were or where they were going. They were walking blind. They were lost. The reason? They had no map.

This isn't uncommon according to Ed Little, a 20-year veteran of search-and-rescue work.

"The biggest problem we have," he says, "is that people don't know the area they're in. Most don't even know the lay of the roads. They not only haven't taken time to look at a map; they often don't even have a map."

Learning to read a map is as important for the outdoorsman as reading a recipe is to the cook. A map is a compact, graphic illustration of the country. Having the appropriate map and knowing how to read it is fundamental to competent outdoors travel.

MAP TERMINOLOGY

These are common terms associated with all map use:

1. *Planimetric map.* Planimetric simply means flat—literally "in one plane." That is, a planimetric map shows no topography. Such a map shows only roads, buildings, campgrounds, lakes, waterways, and other geographical and cultural features. Road maps are planimetric. Maps of public land put out by the U.S. Forest Service, the Bureau of Land Management, and the National Park Service are planimetric. These are valuable navigational tools.

These two kinds of maps can be of great value to you in your outdoor activities. The underneath map, an example of the planimetric type, has a scale of ½ inch to the mile and is published by the U.S. Forest Service. The map on top of it, an example of the topographic type, has a scale of about 1 inch to the mile and is published by the U.S. Geological Survey.

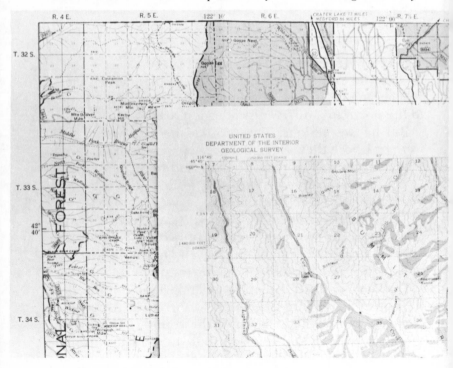

2. *Topographic maps.* These are graphic representations of the earth and are made from aerial photos. They use contour lines to show elevation. Each line represents a specific elevation. From the shape and interval of contour lines, you can identify ridges, peaks, canyons, and other landforms.

3. *Map scale.* The greater the area a map covers, the smaller the scale. A road map that covers an entire state or more is small scale. Some large-scale maps may cover no more than 50 square miles. The larger the scale, the more detail shown.

4. *Map legend.* The legend explains symbols used on a map. On National Forest maps, red lines symbolize primary roads, dotted lines are trails, triangles mean campgrounds, blue means water, and so forth. Symbols may vary. Green on a topographic map represents woodland. On Forest Service maps, green means National Forest land. The legend is printed in the border or in a box at the edge of the map.

5. *Township and range lines.* These are the straight black lines forming a grid on most maps. When land surveys were begun years ago, specific starting points were established throughout the United States. Axis lines were drawn from these points. The east-west axes are called *base lines.* The lines that run north and south are called *meridians.*

Starting at each axis line, additional lines 6 miles apart were surveyed to form townships, areas 6 miles square. The lines running east and west (that is, parallel with the base line) are called *township lines* and are numbered relative to the base line. Thus, the first line above the base line is Township 1 North or, as it's labeled on the map, T. 1 N. Lines running north and south (that is, parallel with the meridian) are called *range lines* and are numbered from the meridian. Thus, the fifth line west of the meridian is Range 5 West, or R. 5 W.

Townships are further divided into sections. A section

is 1 square mile. The 36 sections in each township are numbered, starting in the upper-right corner and running back and forth.

When you do a little map study, this scheme will be clear to you. Understanding survey background is important for finding your way in the field. At the time of surveying, section lines were marked. Perhaps you've seen metal yellow section markers nailed to trees. These plates give a legal description of their locations, that is, they tell township, range, and section. Each marker also has a picture of the township with a nail driven into it. This nail marks the exact position of the tag you're looking at. You can pinpoint your position by comparing the tag with your map. Whenever you're out, keep your eye open for section markers, and practice locating your position on a map by reading the legal description from the marker.

While on a hunting trip, the author pinpoints his position by comparing his map of the area to the marker posted by the Forest Service.

Closeup of the metallic bright-yellow marker shows a combination of printed and scratched-in information. Top and bottom nail hold the marker in place. Third nail is driven in at a point corresponding to location of the tree that holds the marker. (Note that sections within township are numbered starting at the upper right corner and running back and forth, ending in the lower right corner.)

Before going into the field, study maps of your area. Locate campgrounds, ranger stations, and other facilities you may use. Study the road and trail system. Knowing the lay of these routes is essential for easy and safe travel.

Also, study contour lines on your topographic map to learn the nature of the terrain. Reading contour lines is simple. Lines close together represent steep terrain. Lines far apart represent gently sloping ground. Contours in a circle indicate a knob or the top of a mountain. Lines pointing away from high toward lower elevation indicate a ridge; lines pointing from low ground to high represent a draw or canyon. Contour lines can give you an accurate picture of the topography.

You can also get some idea of topography from planimetric maps by studying the relationship of mountains to the networks of streams in various drainages.

Through map study, you can learn the lay of the land before ever seeing a piece of country.

Before setting out, update your maps. On a recent trip, I planned to use topographic maps, but for this area they were based on surveys made in 1950. Forest Service maps for the same country, however, were only 2 years old and showed all the new roads and trails. Prior to the trip, I drew in these new features on my topographic maps, preventing much confusion later.

The kinds of maps you use will vary. If you'll be traveling main highways only, a road map will be adequate. But if your trip will take you to national parks or forests, you'll want larger-scale maps showing back roads and trails, campgrounds, recreation sites, and other details not shown on highway maps. If you're planning an off-road trip, large-scale topographic maps showing small details and terrain are ideal.

Large outdoor stores, surveying-supply shops, and printing shops often carry topographic maps. If you can't get the desired maps there, order them directly from the U. S. Geological Survey. To get a free "order map" of a state (a diagram showing all topographic maps available for that state) east of the Mississippi, write to:

> Branch of Distribution
> U. S. Geological Survey
> 1200 South Eads Street
> Arlington, Virginia 22202

For states west of the Mississippi, write to:

> Branch of Distribution
> U. S. Geological Survey
> Box 25286
> Federal Center
> Denver, Colorado 80225

Order maps give all needed information for buying top-ographic maps.

Maps of federal lands are also valuable. Get in touch with government agencies in your area, or write to regional offices. To get a list of addresses of regional offices, write to the three major federal landholding agencies:

> Director of Information
> U. S. Forest Service
> Washington, D. C. 20250
>
> Chief, Public Affairs
> Bureau of Land Management
> Washington, D. C. 20240
>
> Chief, Media Services
> National Park Service
> Interior Building
> Washington, D. C. 20240

In the field, always have your map along. Carry it where you can get at it easily, but carry it securely. During a heavy snowstorm, Ed Beverly and a friend were relying largely on their map for navigation. Beverly had been tucking the map into a fold inside his cagoule. It slipped out and was lost. Although the two eventually found their way, Beverly stresses that loss of the map could have been disastrous.

A map in constant use can get worn and unreadable. To prevent this problem, cover the map face with clear contact paper, which is thin plastic that has adhesive on one side. You can get such paper at hardware and kitchen-supply stores.

Compass

Half of an effective navigation system is the map; the other half is a compass. Make it a habit to carry these two items.

A compass is basically just a magnetized needle that points in one direction—toward magnetic north. This needle gives you a reference point for determining all other directions. Compasses come in many styles that cost generally from $5 to $25. All compasses do essentially the same thing, but more costly models offer features that make them easier to use. One convenient feature is a liquid-filled (rather than an air-filled) capsule. The liquid stops the magnetic needle quickly and keeps it from oscillating. A compass with a rectangular base is easier to use with a map than is a round compass. Such features as rotating dial, built-in declination setting, and direction-of-travel arrow simplify compass use. Get the best compass you can afford.

COMPASS TERMINOLOGY

A few standard terms apply to all compass use:

1. *Magnetic north.* This is the direction in which the compass needle points. It's different from true (geographic) north, which is at the north pole. The magnetic north pole is in Canada, about 1400 miles south of the geographic north pole.

2. *Declination.* This is the difference in degrees between magnetic north and true north. Declination varies depending on your location. In North America, the line of zero declination runs from Hudson Bay, across Lake Michigan, and down to Georgia. Along this line, the compass needle points toward both true and magnetic north. From any point west of this zero line, the magnetic needle points east of true north. This is easterly declination. From any point east of this line, the compass needle

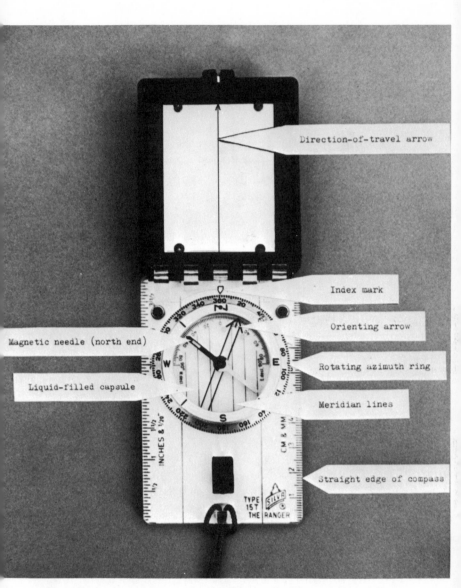

Direction-of-travel arrow

Index mark

Orienting arrow

Magnetic needle (north end)

Rotating azimuth ring

Liquid-filled capsule

Meridian lines

Straight edge of compass

Although one compass may be fundamentally like another, different models have different features. This one, for instance, has a built-in compensator for declination. Here it's set for 20 degrees easterly declination (that is, the orienting arrow is turned to a point 20 degrees east of north). Be sure you study thoroughly the instruction book that comes with your compass. Get lots of practice with compass and map near home before you head for the boondocks.

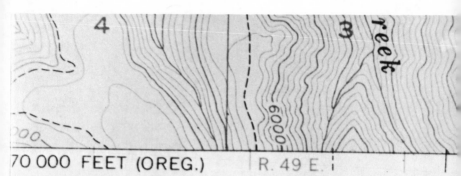

70 000 FEET (OREG.)   R. 49 E.

ological Survey

1
E

lex methods
d check 1954

datum
 system, north zone

d ticks,

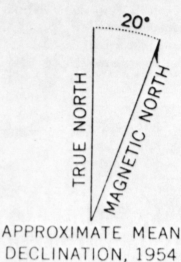

20°

TRUE NORTH

MAGNETIC NORTH

APPROXIMATE MEAN
DECLINATION, 1954

ns

The amount of declination in the area covered by map is printed at the bottom of topographic maps. This map shows a region in the West that has a declination of 20 degrees easterly. If you don't compensate for this amount of declination, you'll be off target nearly a mile after only three miles of travel.

points west of true north. This is westerly declination. If you live in California, declination is easterly; if you live in New York, it's westerly.

3. *Bearing.* This is the direction, or reading, in degrees from one point to another. For example, due east is at a right angle, or 90°, from true north. If you sight across your compass to an object due east, the bearing is 90°.

4. *Azimuth.* This is an angle measured clockwise from the north. Thus, the dial on an azimuth compass is marked in degrees proceeding clockwise from the north. True north is 0° (or 360°), east is 90°, south 180°, and west 270°. The azimuth compass is best for outdoorsmen. Quadrant compasses have a scale divided into four segments of 90° each and are used primarily by surveyors.

In addition to these compass terms, you should know the specific parts of the compass. These are: liquid-filled capsule, direction-of-travel arrow, rotating azimuth ring, orienting arrow, magnetic needle, index mark, meridian lines, and straight edge of compass base. These parts are shown in the accompanying illustration.

Using a compass isn't hard, but it does take practice. You can't learn just by reading about it in this book or anywhere else. Get out your compass and map, and practice each step as you read about it.

All compasses, regardless of style, are used in essentially the same way. The steps described here relate to the popular Silva compasses, which have a rotating azimuth ring. The mechanics of other compasses may differ, but the principle is still the same. Study the direction manual for your compass to learn the specifics of its use.

One end of the magnetic needle is distinct. In the Silva it's painted red. This end always points toward magnetic north. This is the one constant on which all compass use is based.

Fundamentally, a compass enables you to do two things:
• Travel a known direction.
• Learn an unknown direction.

To travel a known direction, rotate the azimuth ring until the desired travel direction lines up with the index mark. For example, if you want to go due east, turn the ring until 90° lines up with the index mark.

Now hold the compass in front of you and turn your body slowly until the orienting arrow comes into line with the magnetic needle. Remember that the north end of the magnetic needle is always the end you line up with the orienting arrow.

Now the direction-of-travel arrow points the way you want to go, that is, due east.

To summarize, for traveling in a chosen direction, you have three check points: 1) set the appropriate degrees mark of the azimuth ring at the index mark; 2) line up the orienting arrow with the north end of the magnetic needle; and 3) follow the direction-of-travel arrow, which tells the direction you want to go.

To learn an unknown direction, you do exactly the opposite. This process is also called taking a bearing. Say you want to learn the direction of a distant peak. Point the direction-of-travel arrow at the peak. Without moving the compass, rotate the azimuth ring until the orienting arrow lines up with the north point of the magnetic needle. Now read the direction of the peak at the index mark.

For example, if the 270° mark on the azimuth ring lines up with the index mark, the peak is due west.

The three check points are the same as for traveling a known direction only in opposite order: 1) point the direction-of-travel arrow toward the object you want to take a bearing on, 2) line up the orienting arrow with the north end of the magnetic needle, and 3) read the direction of the object off the azimuth ring at the index mark.

One point you must keep in mind: If you're working with true direction, you must allow for declination. This principle always applies when you use a compass with a map. Why? Because the map directions are *true* directions

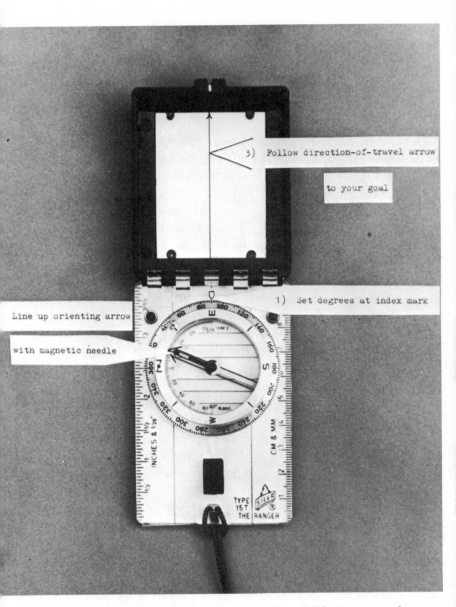

3) Follow direction-of-travel arrow

to your goal

1) Set degrees at index mark

Line up orienting arrow

with magnetic needle

A basic compass use is to travel a known direction. With a compass of this type, the way to travel a known direction (in this instance due east) is to: 1) turn the azimuth ring to line up the 90-degree mark with the index mark, 2) turn the entire compass until the orienting arrow lines up with the magnetic needle, and 3) follow the direction-of-travel arrow, which now points due east, your goal.

and compass directions are magnetic directions. Compensation for declination is important because for every degree of declination error, you'll be off 92 feet in 1 mile of travel.

Assume declination in your area is 20°. If you make no compensation, you'll be off course 1849 feet (more than ⅓ of a mile) in 1 mile's travel. In 3 miles of travel, you'll be off course a full mile.

Declination is shown at the bottom of topographic maps. You can also buy a map showing all declinations for the United States. It's called "Isogenic Chart of the United States, No. I 911." Order it from the U. S. Geological Survey.

You can compensate for declination in either of two ways. The simpler is to buy a compass with a built-in compensating device and to set the appropriate declination for your area on the compass. Just remember that you must reset it if you go to a new area with a different declination.

If your compass has no built-in compensating device, make your own compensator. In essence, you're simply changing the position of the index mark. You can either scratch a permanent mark into the compass base or put a piece of tape on the compass base and make the mark on the tape.

Assume you live in California where declination is 20° easterly. Set the rotating azimuth ring at true north, that is, 0° (this is also 360°) and line up the orienting arrow and the magnetic needle. The direction-of-travel arrow now points toward magnetic north. You want it to point toward true north, however, so scratch a mark on your compass base at the 20° azimuth mark. For easterly declination (which is what the West has), you always *increase* by the amount of declination. That is, in this example, 0° plus 20° equals 20°.

For westerly declination (which is what the East has), you *decrease* by the amount of declination. So if declination

What if your compass has no built-in compensator for declination? Assume you live in California where declination is 20 degrees easterly (as the declination symbol on this topographic map shows). If you make no compensation for declination and you set the compass for true north by setting the zero (or 360) degree mark at the index mark on the compass, the direction-of-travel arrow actually points 20 degrees east of north, toward magnetic north, as it does in this photo. To correct this 20-degree error, make a mark at 20 degrees on the azimuth ring. In this instance, I've put a piece of tape on the compass and made a mark with ink at the 20-degree mark. (Remember, if you live where declination is westerly, say New York, you decrease. If declination in your area is 20 degrees westerly, your mark would be at 340 degrees.)

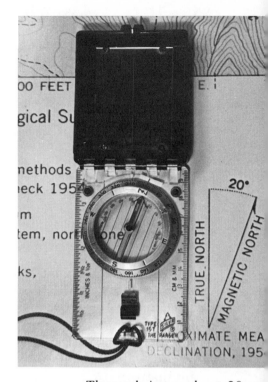

The mark just made at 20 degrees is now the index mark. To align this compass with true north, rotate the azimuth ring so that zero (or 360) degrees is opposite the new index mark on the tape. Now when you line up the orienting arrow with the magnetic needle, the direction-of-travel arrow points true north. To find any true direction, simply align the appropriate degrees mark on the azimuth ring with the new index mark on the tape, and line up the orienting arrow with the magnetic needle. Then the direction-of-travel arrow will be pointing the desired true direction.

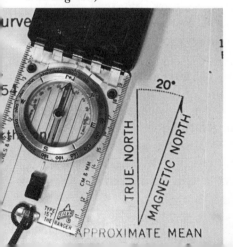

in your area is 20° westerly, your scratch mark would be at 340°. That is, 360 minus 20 equals 340°.

This scratch mark is now your index mark. Rotate the azimuth ring so that zero (true north) is opposite this new mark. Now when you line up the orienting arrow with the magnetic needle, the direction-of-travel arrow points true north.

To find any true direction, follow the same procedure. Simply use the mark you've made on the compass as the index mark.

FUNCTIONS OF THE COMPASS

With these fundamentals in mind, you can put the compass to work in a number of ways. I'll describe four important ones.

1. *Maintaining a straight line of travel.* To keep a straight course by using compass only, aim the direction-of-travel arrow at your destination. This, for example, is a distant point that you can now see but might lose sight of when you begin walking through heavy brush or high trees. Then turn the azimuth ring until the orienting arrow lines up with the magnetic needle. As long as they're in line, the direction-of-travel arrow points toward your goal. Rather than watch your compass constantly as you travel, sight on a landmark, say a tree or rock, on your line of travel. Now put your compass away and walk to that tree or rock. From there, repeat the process. For this purpose you can ignore declination since you're not concerned about true direction.

Using the compass this way is especially valuable when visibility is poor. When Doug Kittredge got caught at night in a heavy fog, he had only to travel a straight line to hit a road that led to camp. But he'd forgot his compass. He tried to stay on course by shining his flashlight from one tree to the next, but with less than 20-foot visibility, he ended up making a perfect 1-mile circle. Eventually he had to spend a cold, miserable night huddled under a tree. Kittredge emphasizes that walking a straight line to hit the road would have been easy with a compass.

2. *To orient a map.* A map that's oriented is one that's lined up to correspond with the earth's surface. If you know where you are and can identify surrounding landforms, you can orient a map simply by visually lining up corresponding features on map and ground.

If you don't know your location or can't identify surrounding features, this isn't possible, so orient the map by using your compass. To do this, set the azimuth ring at true north. Be sure you've compensated for declination on your compass. Lay the compass on the map with the straight edge of the base parallel with the map's north-south lines. Turn the entire map-compass unit until the orienting arrow lines up with the magnetic needle. Now the north-south lines on the map run true north and south. The map is now oriented.

Now you can identify visible but unknown landmarks. I found this technique valuable while hiking to an off-trail lake. The map showed the lake at the base of a cliff, but from my position I could see several similar cliffs and didn't know which one marked the lake. To find out, I oriented the map and compared all visible landmarks with those on the map. By doing this, I was able to identify the cliff nearest the lake. Even with no trail to follow, I found the lake easily.

3. *To tell direction.* If you know you must travel due south, for example, you need only to set your azimuth ring at 180°, line up the orienting arrow and magnetic needle, and the direction-of-travel arrow points due south toward your goal.

Chances are, though, you won't know the exact direction to your goal. To find it, use your map and compass. First, lay the compass on the map and line up the straight edge of the compass base from your present position to your desired destination. Rotate the azimuth ring until the meridian lines in the compass dial parallel the north-south lines on the map. Pick up the compass, hold it in front of you, and turn your entire body until the orienting arrow lines up with the magnetic needle. The direction-of-travel arrow now points toward your desired destination. You can read the direction at the index mark. Again, remember that you must compensate for declination.

4. *To locate your position.* If you don't know where you are but can recognize surrounding topographic features, you can pinpoint your position on the map. Assume you're on a road, river, or other lineal feature but don't know the exact spot and don't know whether to head left or right to camp. You can find your exact location by taking a compass bearing on a prominent landform. If you don't recognize any, orient your map as described above to identify a visible feature. Once you've taken a

One way of pinpointing your position by using map and compass is to take bearings on two known landmarks and from each, draw a line. The point at which the two straight lines cross is your location. Practice near home.

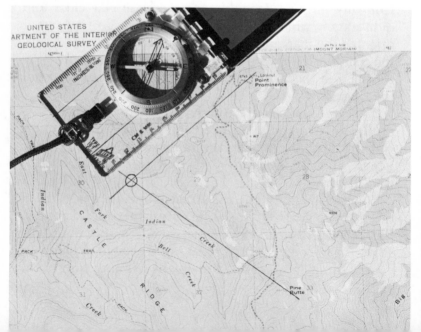

bearing on this feature (as described on page 94) lay the compass on the map with the straight edge of the base touching the feature. Then turn the compass, keeping the edge on that landmark, until the meridian lines of the compass parallel the map's north-south lines. The point at which the straight edge of the base intersects the road or river you're on is your location.

If you aren't on a known lineal feature, you can still pinpoint your location. Follow the same procedure but take bearings on two landmarks and from each of these draw a line along the straight edge of the compass base. The point at which the two lines cross marks your location.

Again, I must emphasize the need to put these procedures into practice. If you simply read how to use a compass and try to figure it out in your mind, it will be only untested theory. But if you have a map and compass in front of you and do each procedure step-by-step as you read, you'll see that the use of map and compass is simple. And in the field, you'll find this knowledge invaluable.

10
RESCUE

A rescue situation is any unplanned occurrence that may alter or end your original plans. You might get lost. You may suffer a broken bone or other incapacitating injury. You may get stranded by deep snow or your vehicle may get stuck in mud or sand. Your car battery may go dead.

If you spend a good deal of time in the outdoors, you'll sooner or later face such emergencies. Under most circumstances, you can help yourself. At other times, you may need outside help. Whether any such incident remains a minor inconvenience or turns into a disaster depends on you: on your initial reaction and your eventual course of action. No two incidents will be the same, so each rescue situation must be handled individually. Nevertheless, some concepts apply generally.

Should You Go Alone?

To say you should never take outings alone is too simple. Some people gain their greatest pleasure from going alone. In some cases, particularly in hunting, the lone outdoorsman is the most efficient. At other times a person may elect to go alone simply because he has no one else to go with.

Whatever the reason, solitary outings are often the best kind. Under many conditions, they present no extraordinary threat to survival. In temperate circumstances, outdoor dangers are minimal. If an emergency occurs, your margin of safety is great. You'll survive long enough to rescue yourself or to be helped by others.

Being alone, though, does heighten the danger of any mishap, particularly injury or illness. If you're with a group, others can give needed assistance. If you're alone, you may be unable to help yourself. Anytime you're planning an outing, consider the level of risk. Under moderate conditions the risk may be minimal, the value of going alone high. At other times the risk may be extreme, overshadowing any benefits of being alone.

The high country in winter is a good example of a high-risk situation. Ed Beverly, a climbing and skiing instructor who often went on outings by himself, stresses this point. One winter he planned to ski around Crater Lake in Oregon. The complete circuit is 34 miles at 8000 feet elevation. He'd planned to go alone, but at the last minute a friend decided to go.

As they set out from the lodge, light snow was falling. The forecast was for clearing, however, so they went ahead, expecting to complete the trip the following afternoon. The first day they made 10 miles and set up camp.

That night, the storm unexpectedly intensified. The next morning, falling snow cut visibility to 100 yards, and the skiers had to break trail through calf-deep snow. The going was slow, and they were forced to camp a second night. That night another 20 inches of snow fell.

"Now the skis wouldn't slide at all," Beverly recalls. "We had to drive our legs with all the power we could muster.

In the deep snow, the skis wanted to head straight up. The tails would fall into the trail just made. It took an hour to cover 100 yards. We traded off breaking trail, but it was bad. The guy in front worked up a sweat while the one in back stood there and froze."

Again they failed to reach the lodge. Soaked, exhausted, and hungry, they set up camp a third night as snow continued to fall. Finally, late the next afternoon, they reached the lodge, two days late.

"The most sobering thought is that I almost went alone," Beverly says. "Under such conditions the energy output just to keep warm is tremendous, but it's even greater to break trail. Without two of us to trade off, it couldn't have been done. In 3½ days I lost 14 pounds, and for 2 years after that I had no tolerance for cold. At that time I decided I'd never take another winter trip alone. Winter conditions are just too unpredictable and overpowering."

Any season or region that presents extremes of cold or hot weather or excessive precipitation must be considered risky for the lone traveler. Country with unusual hazards such as grizzly bears or an abundance of rattlesnakes also should be considered high risk.

Risk increases with the remoteness of the country and the length of a trip. The farther into the backcountry you are and the longer you plan to be gone, the farther you are from help. Also, new country may present unfamiliar dangers. At least for the first trip into any country, travel with someone who knows the area and its dangers.

In any situation, weigh the risks. If they're low, go alone and be cautious. If the risks are high, travel with companions who can help each other during emergencies.

File a Trip Plan

Whatever the circumstances, leave a trip plan with a responsible person—a relative or friend, the sheriff, or a

Always file a trip plan to let someone know your expected travel time and route. If you can't notify a relative or friend, leave a note at your car or at the trailhead.

forest ranger. If this isn't possible, leave a note at your car, or in camp, or at the trailhead, describing your plans. Search-and-rescue unit veteran Dick Suber says people's failure to do this is a major obstacle to helping them in time of trouble.

"We're often called on searches when the only thing the relatives back home know is that the missing person is somewhere between city A and city B, 200 miles away. That doesn't give us much to go on."

An itinerary always should define your travel route and destination. Tell which trails, roads, or drainages you'll take and where you plan to camp. Be specific. Most states have at least a dozen Fish Lakes and Trout Creeks, so give township and range if any possibility for confusion exists.

Also, no one can come to help if they don't know you're overdue, so give your time schedule and stick with it or notify someone of changes. Suber says false alarms are common.

"People say they'll be back at a certain time, but they mean they'll be back, unless such and such happens. They leave out the 'unless' part, so we're out there searching for someone who's off somewhere else, having a good time."

A trip plan should have your name, address, and phone number or this information about someone responsible for you. It also should include your car make and license number and a description of your equipment. If searchers know you have a blue tent and orange pack, they can identify you quickly, even from the air.

How to Handle Emergencies

If you've ever been lost, caught out after dark, trapped in a fog, stuck or stranded, you undoubtedly know the strange, helpless feeling that can grip you. You think about friends worrying back at camp, the dropping temperature of night, hunger, darkness, and natural dangers. You want to run, to do something, anything, fast.

That's the time to stop, take a deep breath, and relax. Right now you need positive thought and action. Panic only causes confusion and aggravates the situation.

"When people suddenly realize they're lost," says Dick Suber, "they don't think. Many just seem to lose their heads and throw common sense to the wind."

You can take steps even now at home to insure a calm attitude under future trying circumstances. First, admit you're not invincible. You can get lost or injured just as anyone else can, and you probably will. If you accept that fact, you won't be stunned when it happens.

Then, prepare for emergencies. Start by putting together a survival kit as described in Chapter 15. Carry equipment to handle the worst you might face. If you're prepared, you'll have no reason to panic. You have everything you need to survive in reasonable comfort.

And, of course, if you've filed a trip plan, you can rest

assured help will be on the way before too long when you don't show up.

What you do in the face of an emergency is as important as advance preparation. First, you should do nothing for a while. Don't act. Rather, sit down for a half hour and think. Ask yourself: Where did I go wrong? How did I get off the trail? Which way was I traveling in relation to the sun? What is the first aid for this injury?

If the weather is cool, build a fire, especially if night is approaching. Darkness in backcountry can be unnerving. The light and warmth of a fire dispels uneasiness and counteracts the feeling of being lost. With a fire, you have a camp. You're at home. This approach applies to any rescue situation. Whether you're injured, stuck, or lost, sit down to think about solutions before diving in with blind action. Action without thought will waste time and energy and often will make things worse.

STAY PUT OR MOVE?

Now that you've made camp and can think, your major decision may be whether to stay where you are or to go on your way. If you're simply disoriented, some reflection may help you get your bearings. If your vehicle is bogged down, you may see a way to get it out. If you've taken a fall but feel all right after an hour's rest, you'll continue on. Most incidents end this way.

But not all. Some may be more serious, and moving could lead to disaster. If you need outside help, the only wise decision is to stay put until help arrives. In trying to decide whether to move, ask yourself some serious questions:

1. *Will I get overtaken by darkness?* Dennis Loomis, a veteran of search-and-rescue missions in Wyoming, says many of his unit's searches are for hunters and hikers who've tried to move at night.

"They end up wandering and really do get lost,"

Loomis says. "If you're caught out at night, stay put. Don't move around. Build a fire. Make camp. In the morning, chances are you'll know right where you are and can walk out. You only make things worse by wandering around at night."

2. *What dangers does the weather present?* Can I find shelter and warmth if I move from my present location? Can I find my way in this fog or falling snow? How far can I travel in this deep snow? Do I have enough water to last to the next water source? Does the country ahead offer protection from the midday sun? If the answers to such questions are negative, the wise choice is to stay where you are.

3. *Are rescue crews looking for me?* If you're not overdue, they probably aren't, so you may decide to proceed. If you're overdue and feel sure someone is looking for you, stay put. A stationary person is much easier to find than one roving about. If you're not sure whether help is on the way and believe you should move, leave a note at your latest campsite describing your travel intentions, and make your trail obvious so searchers can follow you.

4. *Do I know where I'm going and how to get there?* If you don't know the country or where you are, or you don't have a compass or other means of staying on course, you gain nothing by moving.

5. *Am I hurt too badly to move?* If you're physically unable to reach help, trying to move wastes vital energy. Make yourself as comfortable as possible, and settle down to wait for help.

Answers to these and similar questions will depend not only on things such as your physical conditioning and tolerance of pain but also on the size of the party. For example, during darkness, or blizzard conditions, or extremes of heat or cold, the number of people probably makes no difference. No one should move. The party should stay together. On the other hand, if one member were injured, part of the group could stay with the victim while others go for help.

SIGNALLING

If you need help and decide to stay put, you can assist in your own rescue by signalling. In some cases you may signal by sound. At other times, visual signalling may be more effective.

Signalling by sound may involve no more than shouting or firing a rifle to attract attention. These aren't always adequate, however. A person's voice doesn't carry far, and shouting takes a lot of energy. A rifle can be heard a long way, but during the hunting season, most people probably will ignore it.

A more efficient signalling device is a shrill whistle such as police officers use. A whistle takes little energy to blow, and the sound carries a long way. Also, the sound is foreign to outdoors settings, so it attracts attention. Boaters should carry a whistle or horn powered by a pressurized can. These can be heard for a ½ mile or more.

Sight signals are used to attract passing aircraft or to guide ground and air searchers to your position. Flares are effective signalling devices. A big puff of red smoke drifting up through the trees or from the water is easy to see and hard to ignore. Carry flares in boats and back-country vehicles. Most marine-supply stores sell signal flares.

A mirror is good if the sun is shining. The best for this purpose is a military signal mirror. This is a double-sided mirror with a sighting hole in it. Instructions for use are printed on the back. These mirrors are hard to find, but some large surplus stores may still have them.

Otherwise, any small mirror or other shiny reflective object will work. Many compasses have built-in mirrors. To direct a mirror flash to your target, say an airplane, make a V with the fingers of one hand. Hold this hand out toward the target. With the other hand, hold the mirror close to your face under one eye. The process is much like aiming a rifle. The V of the extended hand is the front sight, the mirror is the rear sight. Center the target in the V. Rotate the mirror back and forth until you see its reflected light on the V of the front sight. The flash of the mirror will now hit the airplane. Flip the mirror back and forth to make separate flashes.

Fire is a good signalling method when flares aren't available or the sun isn't shining. At night, the flickering flame can be seen for miles. During the day, smoke from a fire smothered with green leaves or moss will attract attention.

You also can signal with bright clothing, tent, or pack. If you're physically able, use your feet to stamp out letters in an open snow field, or spell out a message with brush or rocks in a visible place. The important thing is contrast and movement. Use the brightest, most contrasting articles you can find, and create movement by waving your arms or tying a flag in the wind. Do everything possible to make yourself visible. Dick Suber says that during one search-and-rescue mission, a lost girl stood quietly under a tree, watching search planes fly over.

Signalling generally is meant only to attract attention. The value of trying to convey specific information is usually questionable, according to search-and-rescue people I've talked with.

"When you try to get across too much, people just get confused," Suber believes. "Most people don't remember the signals anyway. The best approach is to keep signalling simple to avoid confusion.

"But," Suber adds, "you should be able to communicate with a search plane. Once a trained pilot has seen you, he'll fly in the direction you should go. Holding your arms straight out and walking in that direction tells the pilot you're going to walk out. Or you can tell him you're staying put by sitting down or pointing to the ground. The pilot will wag the wings of his plane if he understands."

Some distress signals are standard. If you stamp out the word HELP in the snow, or shout it, the meaning is unquestionable. SOS is a universal distress signal.

Three of anything is accepted as a distress signal. Three fires in a triangle or three puffs of smoke, three blasts on a whistle or three gun shots, three flashes from a mirror, three flags or articles of bright clothing flapping in the breeze—all indicate a need for help.

When should you signal? Use judgment. Signals are wasted if no one hears or sees them. Save your flares until you see or hear an airplane. Don't waste energy shouting blindly. Wait until you hear or see other people. Blowing a whistle takes less energy than shouting, so you might blow three sharp blasts periodically if you think others are in the vicinity.

Of course, you can't always wait until help is within sight to signal. If you're using fires, build them ahead of time, but keep green branches ready to throw on the fire to create smoke when you see or hear an airplane.

11
LIVING DANGERS

The one thing novice outdoorsmen seem to fear most is wild animals. Maybe this notion arises from childhood fairy tales that picture big, bad wolves and bears lurking in the woods, waiting to gobble up little children.

The truth is that wild animals are one of the least fearful aspects of the outdoors. Much more threatening are cold weather, hot weather, lack of water, drowning, and injuries from falls and other accidents. Nevertheless, wild creatures can be dangerous. Bears, venomous snakes, some insects, and spiders, in particular, pose a threat under certain circumstances. But these creatures don't seek out victims. They do their best to avoid human beings and most of them would rather retreat than attack. They demand no fear, only respect and understanding. With a minimum of knowledge, you can enjoy the outdoors without fear of wild animals.

Bears

Under most circumstances, bears stay as far from human beings as possible, but sometimes bears can be aggressive and ferocious. Although bear attacks aren't common, they seem to be increasing. David Richey, an authority on bears, says he has accounts on file of over 50 bear attacks in one two-year period. With increasing interest in outdoors recreation, more people are coming into contact with bears. Also, in many areas the bears are losing their natural fear of man, particularly in parks and campgrounds where they receive handouts or feed at garbage dumps. These bears still have wild dispositions, but they just don't avoid people. The increased contact between bears and people increases the likelihood of bear attacks.

Two species of bears, the black and the grizzly, live in the United States and Canada. Black bears are found throughout the mountainous regions, the Deep South, and across Canada and Alaska. In the East they're black, but in the West their color ranges from black to light cinnamon. Black bears have brown, straight noses, and they have no shoulder hump. Mature black bears weigh from 200 to 400 pounds. A rare huge black bear may weigh over 500 pounds.

In the Lower 48, grizzly bears are rare. Wyoming, Montana, and Idaho have remnant populations concentrated in and around Yellowstone and Glacier National Parks and other deep wilderness. The average grizzly weighs about 400 pounds, an exceptional one, 800 pounds. Grizzlies are usually brown but can be distinguished from brown-colored black bears by the distinct shoulder hump and the concave, dish-shaped nose which is the same color as the body.

All bears are potentially dangerous, but the personality of the grizzly makes him particularly so.

"A grizzly thinks he's king of the country," explains David Richey. "Nothing can conquer him, and he has little

The black bear, though generally not as aggressive as the grizzly, is nevertheless not an animal to take lightly. Identifying signs of the black bear, as this view shows, are a straight nose (which is brown) and lack of a shoulder hump. Black bears may range in color from pure black to light cinnamon. Photo credit: Oregon Department of Fish and Wildlife.

to fear. He's more aggressive than the black bear, and he's unpredictable. You can't say a grizzly will do A or B. You simply must give him as wide a berth as possible."

Regardless of the species, all bears demand respect. In any bear country, follow two rules religiously:

1. *Don't attract bears.* This is a commonly ignored rule. Despite constant warnings from the Park Service, for example, some tourists persist in feeding bears along the roads in national parks. To say the least, the practice is dangerous.

Attracting bears to camp is equally dangerous. In bear country, always keep a clean camp. In particular, don't leave food out. Put it in a plastic bag and hang it high in a tree. Black bears can climb, so hang the food out on a limb where a bear can't reach it. Keep plates and cooking utensils washed, and thoroughly burn garbage or bury it well away from camp and deep enough to seal odors into the ground. Above all, don't store food in your tent or eat in bed. Food odors will attract bears, and tent walls won't keep the animals from coming in to investigate. According to Richey, the sweet smells of perfume and hairspray, as well as odors from menstruation and sexual activity, also attract bears.

2. *Never surprise or corner a bear.* Let bears know you're coming. If you've seen fresh signs—tracks on the trail, broken-up stumps and logs, manure (bear scat is filled with wood chips, hair, and other indigestible matter), scratch marks high on trees—you know bears are near. Make noise. Whistle or talk as you walk. Some experts recommend wearing a bell or rattling a can with rocks in it. Normally, if a bear hears you coming, he'll retreat before you ever see him.

In grizzly country especially, use established trails so you can see ahead. Bears bed down and hunt in dense, off-trail brush where you could surprise one at close quarters. If you see a bear, let him know of your presence from a distance. Get upwind so he can smell you. Chances are he'll leave.

Above all, beware of sows with cubs. Even black bears are aggressive and vicious if their cubs seem threatened. Stay away from cubs, even if the sow isn't in sight.

If you follow these guidelines, probably you will never have bear problems. Despite all caution, however, you may find yourself face to face with a bear someday. According to Richey, any time you're within 50 yards of a bear, your position is critical. The right action could save your life. The wrong one could lose it.

One thing is certain: you can't outrun a bear. For short distances, a bear can outrun a horse. And your running in itself may cause the bear to attack since predatory animals instinctively chase things that run from them.

If you accidentally encounter a bear at close quarters, back away slowly. Don't make quick gestures. Richey says any sudden movement is likely to trigger a charge. If the bear is some distance away, try to locate a tree you can climb. Grizzlies can't climb, but they can reach as high as 10 feet or more, so you must get high. Black bears can climb, but they're less likely to pursue you up a tree than on the ground.

If a bear is within 50 yards and charges, you won't have time to get up a tree. If he just keeps coming, he probably means business. The legend of Davy Crockett notwithstanding, you can no more outfight a bear than you can outrun one. Your screaming or fighting only makes a bear madder and intensifies his rage. Under attack, your only hope is to play dead. Before the bear gets to you, fall to the ground, curl up in a ball, and lock your hands behind your head. In that position, you protect your vulnerable stomach, face, and neck. If you're wearing a pack, it'll help protect your back.

If a bear mauls you and then leaves, lie still for some time. He may hang around to check on you. If he catches you moving, he's liable to attack again. Make sure he's gone before you get up.

Snakes

Each year, about 7000 cases of poisonous snakebite are reported in the United States. On the average, a dozen people die. These figures indicate two things: 1) Snakebite is fairly common, and 2) chances for surviving snakebite are good.

The United States has about 20 species of venomous snakes. Two are coral snakes, one is the cottonmouth, one the copperhead, and the others are rattlesnakes. Only three states—Alaska, Hawaii, and Maine—have no venomous snakes. The states where snakebite is most common are North Carolina, Arkansas, Texas, Georgia, West Virginia, Alabama, Louisiana, Florida, and Arizona.

Copperheads, cottonmouths, and rattlesnakes are pit vipers. The name comes from the depression on each side

This Pacific rattlesnake is giving warning, but many snakes don't. So be observant to avoid trouble. Never peer closely or poke your hands into cracks or crevices where you can't see.

of the head between the eye and the nostril. This "pit" is a heat-receptor organ. These snakes have eyes with catlike, vertical pupils, and they have broad, triangle-shaped heads.

The most dangerous of these is the Eastern diamondback rattlesnake. Its venom is potent, and it's the largest pit viper. Eastern diamondbacks can grow to a length of 6 feet and more. Average maximum length for other rattlesnakes is about 4 feet. Rattlesnakes are found throughout the United States up to 7000 feet elevation in northern latitudes, up to 11,000 feet farther south. All rattlesnake venom is lethal. Antivenin treatment is essential.

Copperheads live throughout the Eastern states in hilly, wooded country in the North, lowlands in the South. Within its range, the copperhead accounts for a majority of snakebite cases, but the bite is rarely fatal. It causes extensive swelling, but antivenin is needed only for small children and elderly people.

Cottonmouths, or water moccasins, inhabit damp areas in the Southern states. They're aggressive, but their venom isn't usually life threatening. Still, cottonmouth bites should be treated with antivenin.

Fewer than one percent of reported snake bites are from coral snakes. The venom, however, is lethal. Symptoms develop slowly, and then the victim is overcome suddenly. Specific antivenin should be given immediately for all bites of a coral snake.

The best snakebite preventive is knowledge. Learn to identify snakes in your area, and know their habits. An excellent book on the subject is *Poisonous Snakes*, available from the U. S. Government Printing Office.

You can't rely on snakes to warn you. Many snakebite victims emphasize that the snakes made no sound before striking. I've encountered personally a number of rattlesnakes that didn't rattle. To avoid trouble, learn where to look and be observant. Snakes are cold-blooded, that is, their body temperature fluctuates with the air temperature. They'll be most active in moderate temperatures. In the cool spring and fall, they'll be out during the day and will lie in the open on sunny rocks, ledges, and other warm spots. At such times, you should stick to cool slopes and shaded areas. If you must be on south slopes and sunny places, move cautiously.

In summer, the situation is reversed. Snakes can't survive for long on hot, sunbaked ground, so they'll seek cooler spots. Most snakes come out at night during hot weather. During the day, they seek shady, protected areas, holes, and burrows.

In cottonmouth country, take care around the stagnant water of marshes, swamps, sluggish creeks, and shallow lakes. In particular, watch branches over water. Also watch logs or rocks where snakes may be basking in the sun, and watch where you're wading.

In any snake country, don't get careless. Before stepping over logs or rocks, look on the far side. A friend of mine one time simply planted his hands on a big log and vaulted over. When he hit the other side his feet missed a 4-foot Pacific rattlesnake by mere inches. Another friend got a good scare while gathering rocks for a fire pit. He stuck his fingers under a rock and lifted it to find a big rattlesnake coiled up underneath. Never poke your fingers into places you can't see, and don't peer from close range into crevices and holes.

Finally, don't tease snakes or go out of your way to kill them. By doing so you only set yourself up for trouble. The best policy with snakes, as with bears, is to give them a wide berth.

In snake country, sleep in a tent with a zippered door. And while hiking there, wear boots with tops high enough to cover the ankle, where most snakebites occur. A snake's fangs can't penetrate heavy leather.

If you or one of your party does get bitten by a snake, the first action is to determine if any venom has been injected. According to Dr. Findlay Russell, director of neurological research at the Los Angeles County-University of Southern California Medical Center, many cases of snakebite are the work of nonvenomous snakes, and venomous snakes sometimes inject no venom. He says he's seen a number of snakebite victims who've received no venom.

He observes all patients for four hours. If no symptoms arise, he releases them without treatment. Treating a person who's received no venom is dangerous, he says.

The venomous bite will produce an almost instant burning pain. Usually the area around the bite will swell markedly within 10 minutes. Within an hour, the entire limb may swell. In severe cases, the victim's mouth and tongue will have a numb, tingling sensation. The person may be weak, sweating, or nauseated, and he may faint.

Dr. Russell, who has attended more than 675 cases of snakebite, puts little faith in first-aid measures.

"If you don't do anything, you at least haven't done anything wrong," he says.

If you're no more than 30 to 40 minutes from a hospital, according to Russell, the best course of action is to immobilize the bitten part, keep the victim calm with comfort and reassurance, and get him to the hospital for antivenin treatment. Getting any snakebite victim to a hospital, he says, is always the most important step in treatment.

If you're more than 40 minutes to an hour from a hospital, first-aid treatment may have some value, Russell says. Treatment should begin quickly, preferably within 15 minutes. If delayed more than 30 minutes, according to Russell, first aid is of little or no value. The victim simply should be kept calm and taken to a hospital.

The objectives of first aid for snakebite are: 1) to remove as much venom as possible, and 2) to slow the spread of venom. Begin by placing a constricting band 2 to 4 inches above the bite, that is, between the bite and the body. A strip of cloth or a rubber band works well. This band restricts venom flow through the lymph system. It's *not* a tourniquet to stop blood flow, so it must not be tight. You should be able to slip a finger under it easily. According to Russell, this band need not be loosened or removed since it does not restrict the flow of blood.

Next, using the sterile blade in a snakebite kit or a knife or razorblade sterilized in a flame or in alcohol, make incisions about ¼ inch long and no more than skin deep, about ⅛ inch, through the fang marks. Make only one incision, parallel with the limb, through each mark. With snakebite-kit suction cups, or with your mouth if it has no open sores, suck venom from the slits. Spit it out. Continue this sucking process for about a half-hour.

Russell says this process may remove as much as 10 to 15 percent of the venom.

When you're ready to move the victim, splint the injured limb to minimize movement. If the person must walk, he should move slowly and calmly. Take him to the hospital for antivenin treatment.

If possible, kill the snake with a long stick, with a rock, or by shooting, and take it along. Venom differs from one species to another. Doctors must know the exact species in order to give the most effective treatment.

Antivenin treatment isn't recommended as a first-aid measure. Antivenin is a horse serum to which some people suffer allergic reactions. They may die quickly from this reaction if not under hospital care.

A person bitten by a snake should *not* drink alcohol. Alcohol dilates the blood vessels, increasing circulation and the spread of venom. Most doctors advise against the use of ice or chemical cold packs in treating snakebite. Extreme cold may cause excessive tissue damage.

Spiders, Insects, and Scorpions

The black widow is probably the best known and most widely distributed venomous spider. Black widows have round, shiny-black bodies about ½ inch long with the red "hourglass" on the underside. Including legs, a black widow may be 2 inches long.

To avoid spiders, watch for webs. Black-widow webs have no apparent pattern. The center is a tunnel of silk hidden in a dark crack or hole at the top of the web. The spider hides here during the day. From this hideaway, a maze of strands radiates down and out, getting more sparse toward the bottom. Webs are built in house corners, animal burrows, crevices in the soil, rock piles, and stacked wood or lumber.

Black widows are retiring and shy. They don't attack.

The black widow is widely distributed and fairly common. This one, shown hanging upside down from its web, is a female. Overall measure, including legs, is about 2 inches. Bite of black widow is rarely fatal for adults, but it can kill a child or an elderly person.

The danger lies in the possibility of getting a spider in your clothing, or in picking up a piece of wood or a rock and squeezing the spider against your body. It will then bite in self-defense.

A black-widow bite feels like a sharp pinprick, but the bite marks aren't obvious. Little or no swelling occurs. Within about 15 minutes, acute pain develops and spreads rapidly, finally affecting the entire abdomen with cramping, possibly excruciating pain. Symptoms may include nausea, faintness, tremors, sweating, slurred speech, and shock.

A black-widow bite probably won't kill a healthy adult. The venom is perhaps 15 times as potent as that of most rattlesnakes, but the volume is small. Normally the pain begins to subside within hours, and after 2 to 3 days the symptoms disappear.

According to Dr. Findlay Russell, who's seen nearly as many cases of black-widow bite as he has snakebite, no effective first aid exists for spider bites.

"It's best that a person do nothing," Russell says. "First-aid attempts only confuse the diagnosis."

Although a black-widow bite may not kill a healthy adult, it could be lethal for small children, and also for elderly people, especially those with a history of cardiac or respiratory problems. These people, as well as pregnant women and anyone else with acute symptoms from the bite, should be hospitalized for possible antivenin treatment.

Snakes and spiders bite, but bees and wasps sting. The stinger is located at the rear of the body. Stinging is a defensive act meant to drive away danger. It can be very painful. A bee sting may seem insignificant, but many people are allergic to stings. For them, a sting can be deadly.

Normally, bees won't sting unless stepped on or caught in clothing and squeezed. To avoid bee stings, don't go barefoot in flowery places, and watch where you sit down and put your hands. If you do get stung by a bee, the stinger probably will remain in your skin. Don't try to pull it out, an action that forces more poison into your skin. Scrape the stinger out with a knife blade.

Wasps, particularly yellow jackets and hornets, are aggressive around their nests. The nests are often grey "paper" sacks hanging in trees, or they may be in the ground, or in rotten logs. Be alert for the hanging nests or for insects hovering close to the ground. Stay away from those places. If you see one nest, watch carefully for others. In the high Sierras, I got into an area of willow trees and meadows infested with yellow jackets. I counted more than two dozen nests.

Bee and wasp stings, as well as stings of the fire ant—an introduced species now found throughout the Deep South—can be fatal within minutes for persons allergic to

This yellow jackets' nest in the branch of a conifer resembles a gray paper bag. Yellow jackets are aggressive in protecting their nest, so keep your distance. Anybody allergic to insect stings should carry emergency medication.

them. According to Dr. Ken Magee, persons who have suffered severe breathing difficulties or hivelike swelling from stings in the past can assume they're hypersensitive to insect stings. Hypersensitive individuals should carry a kit containing epinephrine and an antihistamine wherever the possibility of getting stung exists. The kit is obtained by prescription.

Scorpions also sting. Only one species in the United States is dangerous. It's found in New Mexico and Arizona and along the Colorado River in California. This scorpion has caused enough deaths in Mexico—1500 in one year, according to Dr. Russell—that the nation has developed a specific antivenin.

The symptoms of scorpion stings are immediate pain, numbness, and tingling in the affected area. An affected limb may become weak and hypersensitive to touch. Scorpion stings require no specific first-aid treatment. But if the reaction is severe, which is likely in children, the victim should be taken to the hospital for antivenin treatment.

Scorpions seek dark hiding places. In scorpion country, sleep in a bug-proof tent. And before you put on shoes and clothing, shake them out to make sure no scorpions have decided to spend the day there.

12
VEHICLE SAFETY

This chapter deals specifically with automobile and snowmobile safety, but the same principles apply to all vehicle use. Whether you ride a motorcycle, bicycle, or an all-terrain vehicle, the emphasis for safety should be on preplanning. Prepare for potential mechanical problems. Make a pretrip inspection of your equipment, and carry tools and spare parts to handle common mechanical problems in the field. And always carry survival gear equal to the worst conditions you may encounter. Complete lists of survival gear for use in automobiles and snowmobiles can be found in Chapter 15.

Automobile Safety

The place to begin vehicle safety is with sound equipment. Prior to any trip, look over your rig. These are the major checkpoints:

1. *Gasoline.* Start with a full tank and fill up at every opportunity. For backroad travel, carry a spare 5-gallon

For insurance against getting stuck or stranded, nothing beats good judgment. Learn the limitations of your vehicle, and also carry the proper emergency equipment.

can of gasoline. The gasoline should be in a heavy-duty jeep can that's held tight so it can't be thrown loose on rough roads.

2. *Fluid levels.* Check the battery-fluid level. Make sure the cooling system is full and that antifreeze offers adequate protection.

3. *Oil.* Oil should be at the proper level and of the right weight. For easier starting, use a lighter-weight oil in winter than in summer.

4. *Brakes.* Adjust brakes so they don't pull or grab, a dangerous trait especially on slick roads. Check brake-fluid level. Make sure the parking brake works properly.

5. *Exhaust system.* During winter, windows will be closed, so having a tight exhaust system is important to prevent carbon-monoxide fumes from leaking into the cab.

6. *Heater and defroster.* These are essential for warmth and a clear view.

7. *Lights.* Good headlights and taillights play a big part in safe driving at night and in fog or snow.

8. *Windshield.* Install good wiper blades, and use anti-freeze in the windshield washer.

9. *Tires.* Replace worn tires to avoid blowouts and flats. Snow tires should have plenty of tread for maximum traction.

Check these items yourself before any trip. If you have little mechanical knowledge, have a mechanic inspect and repair other parts periodically. Billie Chambers, who is active in Western four-wheel drive clubs, says his club's members give their vehicles a complete mechanical check-up every 3 months. In addition to checking most of the points I've already mentioned, they inspect moving parts such as wheel bearings, universal joints, and ball joints or kingpins.

The engine also should be tuned regularly for easy starting and efficient running.

Automobile emergencies probably occur most frequently from breakdowns, getting stuck, and getting stranded by heavy weather. Regular maintenance as just

In desolate country such as this, help could be a long time coming in an emergency. So extra water and rations, as well as other emergency equipment and supplies, are vital for safe travel.

described is the major preventive of breakdowns. Some mechanical problems can be repaired in the field if you prepare by assembling and carrying the needed equipment.

The defense against getting bogged down and stuck is good judgment. As Billie Chambers puts it, "Just having a four-wheel-drive doesn't mean you can go anywhere. You have to use judgment."

To avoid getting hopelessly bogged down, test water holes and mud before crossing. Don't try to plow through snow deeper than the axles. Stay off loose sand. If you're going to push your vehicle to the extreme, do it when you're with other rigs so that help is at hand. Use extra caution when you're alone.

Search-and-rescue records in Oregon show frequent rescue missions to help motorists who've gone into the backcountry in fair weather only to be stranded by 2 or 3 feet of fresh snow from a major storm. Getting a professional forecast before going into remote country is one way to avoid such an emergency. But as Chapter 2 makes clear, no forecast guarantees immunity to weather problems.

When a sudden snowstorm or blizzard does catch you, or you're stranded by other circumstances, survival may ride on your course of action. Chapter 10 gives suggestions for deciding what to do. If you know the country and conditions are moderate, you might decide to go for help. But often threatening conditions will dictate that you stay with your vehicle to wait for help.

For example, you may have a breakdown or get bogged down in loose sand in the desert where midday temperatures are over 100° F. and you're 20 miles from help. You'd be foolish to set out walking. Stay with your rig where you have a water supply or at least materials for constructing a simple desert still. The vehicle itself will provide shade. And most important, rescue crews can spot your vehicle much more easily than they can spot you alone.

The same line of reasoning holds true if you're trapped by a blizzard or heavy snow. Your vehicle will be found most quickly, and it guarantees shelter from wind and snow. And as long as fuel lasts, the heater assures warmth.

In a blizzard, snow will accumulate faster than you can shovel it away, so don't exhaust yourself fighting elements you can't beat. Save your energy to keep warm. Run the engine to heat the car only for short periods and crack windows on the downwind side for ventilation. Get out occasionally to clear drifted snow away from the tailpipe. Dennis Loomis recounts a blizzard rescue near Sheridan, Wyoming, where drivers failed to do this.

"We had to rescue 22 people right off the interstate highway," Loomis says. "Snow was coming down so fast that crews couldn't keep the road plowed open.

"The real problem was that a lot of people were sick from carbon-monoxide poisoning. Very sick. Three-foot drifts were building up in 20 minutes. People were running their engines to stay warm, but they didn't get out to clean snow away from the exhaust pipes. Fumes were backing up into the cars."

To guard further against the insidious danger of poisoning, have at least one person in the vehicle stay awake at all times.

Snowmobile Safety

Snowmobiles present problems that other motorized vehicles don't. For one thing, they lack any "relief" factor. A motorcycle or car, for example, continues to roll when the throttle is shut down, but a snowmobile stops. To keep moving, it must be under power. This characteristic, coupled with the fact that the machine is ridden over rough, unpredictable ground, makes breakdowns fairly common.

As in dealing with other vehicles, the place to begin prevention of mechanical problems is at home, before a trip. As Don Stonehill, a snowmobiling safety instructor, says, "Snowmobilers always should pull a preflight maintenance check just as pilots do."

Stonehill suggests the following checkpoints:

1. *Drive belt.* Look for weak spots and wear. Drive belts undergo a lot of stress and can break. A broken belt puts a machine out of operation.

A big factor in snowmobile safety is a pre-trip inspection of equipment. Here is Don Stonehill checking the drive belt on his snowmobile for wear.

2. *Spark plugs.* Snowmobile engines require oil mixed with the fuel for engine lubrication. The oil can foul plugs. Replace fouled plugs with new ones.

3. *Steering system.* Make sure it's working properly, and inspect skis for broken or loose parts.

4. *The track.* Check the alignment, and look for broken or loose parts in the suspension system.

5. *Gasoline.* Start with a full tank. As Stonehill says, "In 10 feet of snow, 20 miles from nowhere is no place to think about checking your fuel. Always start out with a full tank."

A maintenance check may get you off to a good start, but it's no guarantee against breakdown. You may have to deal with mechanical problems in the field. Chapter 15 gives a recommended list of equipment and parts that should be carried in the field.

One of the best safety measures for snowmobilers is to travel in groups. In case of a breakdown, help is available.

To further insure safety while snowmobiling, Stonehill recommends the following precautions:

1. *Travel in groups.* On a snowmobile, you can get miles from the nearest road in little time. If your machine breaks down, you're stuck unless you have companions to tow you out or to give you a ride to safety. Travel with at least one other machine and, better still, in a party.

2. *File a travel plan.* This is discussed fully in Chapter 10.

3. *Use extra caution in new areas.* Riding at high speed in unfamiliar country is dangerous, as a couple of examples make clear. In one case, a man gunned his machine across an open flat in the Cascade Mountains, not realizing that a ditch ran through the flat. When he hit the ditch, his machine plowed into the opposite bank, catapulting the rider over the handlebars. The windshield caught him just under the nose. He wasn't killed, but 20 stitches were required to sew his nose back on.

In another incident, a man and wife were riding tandem in an unfamiliar area. They drove over a 20-foot cliff, and the woman suffered a chronic back injury.

4. *Stay with your machine in an emergency.* If you follow rule one, party members can help each other. But severe conditions may strand an entire group, or under unusual circumstances, you may get caught out alone. In either case, stay with your machine.

For one thing, a snowmobile track is much easier to follow than footprints. When searchers set out, they can follow that track directly to you.

Just as important, the machines provide survival resources. They can serve as windbreaks. Or you can use a cowling as shelter or as a shovel to dig a snow shelter. As long as you're with a machine, you have gasoline for fire starting. Even if the tank is empty, you can use a rag to soak up fuel from the fuel line or carburetor. Be careful. Gasoline is explosive. Never pour gasoline onto a fire.

If a search is on but you are hidden in a canyon or dense forest, Stonehill suggests that you turn over a snowmobile and set the track on fire to send up a black smoke signal. The practice is hard on snowmobiles, but it's better than freezing to death.

5. *Don't drink while snowmobiling.* Taking a leather bag of wine is popular, but it can be dangerous. Even a small amount of alcohol makes a person less cautious than normal. Foolish stunts, especially in winter, can be deadly.

Also, contrary to popular belief, a stiff drink doesn't warm a person but rather increases the rate of chilling.

6. *Learn to ride properly.* Stonehill says that riding a snowmobile involves certain moves that can be learned only through training and experience. He recommends that beginners take part in a snowmobiling safety clinic and ride with experienced friends.

7. *Wear proper clothing.* A snowmobile rider does little physical exercise to generate body heat, and the fast movement of the machine creates a wind-chill problem. Buy clothing made specifically for snowmobiling.

Proper clothing is a big part of snowmobiling safety. The ideal outfit to wear while under way is a special snowmobile suit plus a helmet for protection and warmth and a face shield to protect the eyes from wind and blowing snow.

Boots, gloves, and headgear are critical items. Snowmobile boots are made of wind-resistant nylon with thick felt liners. Most snowmobile riders wear leather gloves with heavy insulation or wool gloves with an outer wind shell of nylon or leather.

For maximum head protection and warmth, wear a helmet. Stonehill recommends a full-face helmet that covers the entire head except for the eyes. Wear either goggles or a face shield to protect eyes from the wind and blowing snow.

Wear a snowmobile suit made of windproof, water-resistant material with a pile lining. Zippers on these suits are covered to block wind, and the cuffs and wrists are tightly knit to keep out snow. A high liner prevents snow from falling down the neck.

Snowmobilers shouldn't wear a scarf or other loose clothing that can get caught in moving parts of the machine.

13
BOATING SAFETY

In this chapter, guidelines are primarily for use on inland lakes and rivers. Craft used may range from runabouts to cartop fishing boats to canoes, johnboats, dinghies, and rubber rafts. Boaters going onto oceans, the Great Lakes, and large developed rivers should have more specialized knowledge and training.

Activities on water present problems and dangers not associated with activities on land. The margin of error is often small. A major reason is the rapid chilling effects of water. According to studies conducted at the University of Victoria (B. C.), survival time for the average adult in 50° F. water is less than 3 hours, in 32° F. water, less than 1½ hours. Water must be warmer than about 80° F. before body cooling is no longer a problem.

Options are few in water. You can't build a shelter or make a fire, you can't lie down to rest or sleep, nor can you put on more clothes to stay warm. You must work continuously to stay afloat or to swim to shore, and the only way to get warm and stay warm is to get out of the water. Water offers little leeway for the accident victim.

135

This rubber raft might be great for fishing small lakes high in the mountains, but it shouldn't be used on large, open waters. Always operate within the safety limits of whatever craft you use.

Boating Accidents

1. *Capsizing and swamping.* To capsize is to have your boat overturn. To swamp is to have your boat sink by filling with water. Swamping and capsizing are the most frequent causes of boating fatalities in the United States. These accidents occur in several ways.

One common cause is turning too fast, especially on rough water. Small, lightweight boats aren't designed for high-speed turns, and they flip easily. If your boat bounces or lurches as you turn, you're going too fast.

Collisions also cause many capsizing and swamping accidents. According to Tom Poore, a Navy veteran and safety instructor for the U. S. Coast Guard Auxiliary in Oregon, many collisions are the result of recklessness.

"Many boaters push their boats too fast in restricted areas where chances of a collision are great," Poore has observed, "and most don't maintain a proper lookout."

The deadly result can be collisions with other boats, pilings, docks, and floating debris.

Another frequent cause of collisions is ignorance of the rules of the road. Marina operator Steve Byman says that very few boat operators know these rules.

"Not only is this knowledge essential for safe boating,"

Byman points out, "but also it's legally required. A person can be cited on the water just as he can on the highway."

Rules of the road for boating are similar to those for automobiles. If two boats are approaching port-to-port (that is, left side to left side), they should hold their course. If approaching head on, they each should swing right to pass port-to-port. However, if they're approaching starboard-to-starboard (that is, right side to right side) they need not cross to each other's left but should continue on course.

When two boats approach each other at about a right angle, the boat on the right, just like a car on the right at an intersection, has the right of way. The driver should maintain course and speed while the boat on the left slows to pass behind.

When one boat is overtaking another, the boat in front is privileged and should maintain course and speed. The overtaking boat should swing out to pass. Sailboats and craft being rowed or paddled have the right-of-way over motorboats. Every boater is responsible for his own wake and is liable for any damage it causes. A large wake can swamp nearby small boats.

Tom Poore says another cause of swamping that he observes frequently is overloading. Every boat, he stresses, has a load capacity that should be observed strictly. A metal plate, usually on the transom, tells this capacity. The results of ignoring the recommended weight limit can be fatal. During a recent March, three men set out on a lake in southern Oregon with their 16-foot boat powered by a 45-horsepower outboard. The boat was heavily loaded with camping gear and firewood. As the wind came up, the boat swamped. All three men died.

Rough water, as well as overloading, probably contributed to that accident. Before you set out on a boat trip, especially on large lakes where the safety of shore may be miles away, get a weather forecast. Don't push your luck with high winds.

If you do much boating, sooner or later you'll get caught by rough water. Learning to handle a boat in rough conditions is largely a matter of feel and experience, but a few guidelines are helpful. For one thing, don't run directly into or sideways to large waves that could flip or swamp your boat. Instead, quarter into the waves and throttle down to prevent the boat's bucking or plowing into waves. Avoid running with the wind, especially in a small boat with a low transom. Waves can wash over the back and fill the boat. If you have no choice but to run with the wind, hold a speed that keeps your boat moving just ahead of the waves, being careful not to plow into swells ahead.

If your motor dies, or you run out of fuel in rough water, or the water is just too heavy for safe running, the best choice may be to throw out a sea anchor and drift. A sea anchor is simply a drag to keep the boat headed into the wind. A bucket, a tackle box, a shirt with the neck and sleeves knotted, anything that will fill with water to create drag, will work. Tie this off the bow with 20 to 30 feet of line.

In any rough water, distribute cargo weight evenly across the floor of the boat. Have all passengers sit on the bottom, keeping the center of gravity as low as possible to minimize tipping.

2. *Falling overboard.* Falling overboard is another major cause of boating fatalities. Passengers should never ride on the bow or sides of the boat. A jolt from waves or the wake of another boat could throw them into the water. In a small boat, passengers should stay seated while the boat is moving. In any boat, the operator should never accelerate or make sharp turns suddenly if a passenger is standing.

Many boating accidents are the result of drinking. On Klamath Lake in southern Oregon during two recent years, four persons drowned after falling overboard. Drinking was involved in each case. According to Dr. John

S. Hayward of the University of Victoria (B. C.), about ⅓ of all boating fatalities involve drinking.

Steve Byman has taken part in many search missions involving drunken boaters. Frequently the unobservant operators simply have run out of fuel. Others have run their boats completely onto dry land. Byman estimates that 75 percent or more of the boaters who come through his marina have been drinking.

"Drinking and boating seem to go together," Byman says. "Some people come in here so stewed they can hardly walk up the dock, yet they're still driving their boats. Drinking while boating is a very dangerous practice."

3. *Fires and explosions.* According to Byman, fires and explosions are the number-one cause of boat damage in the United States. Most of these accidents occur during fueling.

If possible, remove the tank from the boat when you get fuel. On boats with built-in tanks, close all hatch and cabin doors before fueling to prevent gas fumes, which are heavier than air, from settling into low areas. After fueling, open hatches and turn on blowers to purge fumes from the boat. Don't smoke around fuel docks or gas tanks. Even on water, gasoline burns. Byman says that one time a little gasoline overflowed into the water as a boater filled his built-in tank. The man didn't notice and lit a cigarette, then flipped the match onto the water. The water around the boat exploded into flame. No one was killed, but the boat was charred.

HANDLING ACCIDENTS

Despite all caution, you still may have a boating accident. Knowing what to do can save lives.

Regardless of conditions, children and nonswimmers who go boating should wear life jackets. When conditions are threatening, everyone should wear a life preserver.

Children and nonswimmers should wear life jackets whenever they're on the water. Boaters must be particularly conscious of safety because water involves dangers not associated with land activities.

If you're alone and fall overboard, the wind may push your boat out of reach. Don't waste energy swimming after it. Catching a wind-blown boat is nearly impossible. You should either head for shore or (if a chance for rescue exists) assume a floating position to save as much energy as possible as you wait for help.

Standard advice when a boat swamps or capsizes is to stay with the craft. It will float and hold you up. Even if it's partially submerged, a boat is easier for rescuers to spot than an isolated head bobbing in the waves.

If the water is exceptionally cold and chances for being rescued within a couple of hours are slim, your only hope may be to swim for shore. This is a desperation move, however. If you have more than a mile to go, you probably won't make it. Hypothermia will overcome a swimmer in cold water quickly as the movements of swimming pump fresh, cold water through his clothing and draw heat away rapidly. In cold water, a person can't generate enough body heat through exercise to replace heat lost through conduction to the water.

In one accident, the boat of three duck hunters swamped. One man tried to swim to shore. Although he was a strong swimmer and had only a ¼ mile to go, he didn't make it. He was overcome by hypothermia. The two other hunters stayed with the boat and were rescued about a half hour later. According to studies of hypothermia, *swimming* in cold water reduces survival time by about ⅓.

If a person remains still, water trapped in his clothing will warm slightly and slow heat loss. The head, the sides of the chest, and the groin area are the major points of heat loss. To slow chilling, an accident victim in cold water should hold his head out of the water and pull himself into a ball by holding his arms tight against his sides to reduce heat loss from the armpits and by drawing his legs up to keep water from circulating across the groin, a major area of heat loss. A person on a swamped or capsized boat should keep as much of his body out of the water as possible.

If you spend a lot of time on water, more specialized boating knowledge may be valuable. Two books put out by the American National Red Cross and available at Red Cross offices are good. They are: *Basic Outboard Boating* and *Basic Rescue and Water Safety*. Another Red Cross book called *Canoeing* goes into the fine points of that sport.

To prevent emergencies and to signal for help when emergencies arise, all craft should have safety and distress equipment aboard. See Chapter 15 for a list of recommended equipment.

Whitewater Safety

The principles discussed so far apply to boating generally, but rivers present problems that must be considered specifically. Doug Shorey has run many Western rivers, including the Salmon and Snake Rivers in Idaho, the

Owyhee in Oregon, and many smaller rivers, both by canoe and as a professional rafting guide. The following suggestions come largely from Shorey's experience:

1. *Wear a life jacket.* "This is the oldest rule in the book," Shorey says, "but it's often ignored. River currents are just too strong and unpredictable for even the strongest swimmer. No one can successfully fight a heavy river. Besides, you might get tangled in ropes, or heavy clothing could pull you under. You might bump your head on a rock. In these cases, your only protection against drowning is that life preserver.

Only after you become totally familiar with your canoe or kayak in gentler waters should you start to use it in white water. And then you should observe one of the oldest rules in the book: wear a life jacket.

The place to learn your canoeing skills is in gentle waters close to home. Remember: the canoe will float even if it swamps, so stay with it.

"Another thing we always told clients on the Salmon is not to try to swim, even downstream. The current is much too powerful," Shorey says. "Instead, a person in the water should hold hands and feet straight out in front and drift. This way you'll bounce off rocks feet first and can gradually work your way to shore in a calmer place."

If you go overboard, try to stay on the upstream side of your canoe or raft to avoid being crushed between it and rocks or other objects.

2. *Carry extra paddles and oars.* Shorey says he's gone through as many as three canoe paddles on one trip. He always carries two spares. For rafting, he recommends two extra oars, which should be tied in a handy location. The best place is probably inside the tubes, where they won't be smashed if the raft hits a rock.

3. *Know your equipment.* Before tackling dangerous rivers, learn the nature of your equipment and how to handle it.

"We've run into lots of people on the Salmon River who've never run whitewater before," Shorey says. "A river like that is no place to learn. The guides and experienced boatmen spend half their time fishing novices out of the river and rounding up their equipment.

"Many people don't even know how to inflate a raft. We watched one party hit Owl Creek Rapids on the Middle Salmon River. Their raft was too soft. When it hit a big wave, it buckled and folded in half. Then it flipped over backwards. None of the four passengers even had on a life jacket. None drowned, but it was a miracle."

The place to learn, Shorey emphasizes, is on easy water where mistakes don't threaten your life. Learn how to load and balance the craft, learn the paddle strokes, adjust oars to fit you, and learn how to read currents and to handle emergencies. Practice canoeing with your partner to develop teamwork.

"When you make your first whitewater trip, whatever your craft, go with someone experienced," Shorey advises. "Working whitewater is a lot different than smoother water."

4. *Know the river.* This is as important as knowing your equipment. Putting in at the top and heading down blindly is foolhardy. Shorey says studying maps of the river should be the first step. Maps showing rapids and giving classifications are available for many major rivers.

Then talk to anyone and everyone you can find who's run the river. Pick their brains concerning specific rapids and other spots that might be tough to run.

"And remember," says Shorey, "that a river may be completely different in June than in August, and from one year to the next. Keep this in mind as you plan."

Finally, as the trip progresses, stop to scout ahead, especially if you can't see the water ahead. Look for overhanging trees or log jams that could give trouble, and examine currents to develop alternate plans for going

It's just as important to know the river as it is to know your equipment. Remember that a river can vary from season to season and from year to year. Study maps and talk to people who have traveled it.

through. If plan A fails, you'll want a plan B; if that one doesn't work you'll need a plan C and so forth.

5. *Ride safely.* On fast or rough water, canoeists should kneel to lower the craft's center of gravity and to place weight on the bottom of the boat for stability. Raft passengers should ride inside, not on the tubes, and they should keep arms and legs inside where they can't be crushed between the raft and rocks.

6. *Insure dry equipment.* Vital items such as sleeping bags and clothing should be double-wrapped in heavy plastic garbage bags. Wet clothing and sleeping gear will be uncomfortable and, in cold weather, deadly as well. Shorey says his practice of always carrying spare clothing saved his life one time while he was hunting ducks by canoe.

"The temperature was below zero when I accidentally

filled the canoe half full of water. I pulled to shore quickly and changed clothes and went ahead with the trip. Without those clothes I'd have been in trouble."

7. *Stop before dark.* On overnight trips, plan campsites carefully so you're able to shut down in daylight. Reading currents is essential for safety. In bad light, the potential for accidents increases drastically.

8. *Don't boat alone.* You may capsize and lose your equipment, or you may need help getting out of paralyzingly cold water.

14
FIRST AID

The belief seems to be widespread that modern hospitals and transportation equipment will solve all medical problems. Surrounded by technological marvels, people can easily become complacent. Modern technology will offer little comfort, however, if you've just broken your leg 10 miles from the nearest road. You're suddenly thrust back to a primitive age. Advanced technology is forgotten. Survival now depends strictly on what you know and do.

And this depends on your first-aid knowledge. Not everyone can attend medical school to learn advanced medical treatments, but everyone can and should know first-aid fundamentals for common outdoors injuries. This chapter covers these fundamentals, the minimum knowledge needed for everyday outings. Persons involved in extended backcountry trips and expeditions, where medical aid may be days or weeks away, should have advanced training.

Principles of First Aid

Regardless of circumstances, certain first-aid principles (main ideas) always apply. If you know these principles, you're equipped to deal with most first-aid emergencies. First I'll list the principles. Then, in following sections, I'll cover specifics for carrying out these principles.

1. *Stop major bleeding.* Rapid blood loss can kill a person in less than 3 minutes. Preventing such loss should be the first life-saving step.

2. *Restore breathing.* If breathing has stopped, a person can suffer major brain damage from lack of oxygen within 5 minutes. This is the second life-saving step.

3. *Treat for shock.* A person's injuries may not be extensive, but he still can suffer shock, a life-threatening complication. In giving first aid for all serious injuries, always treat for shock.

4. *Prevent further injury.* This may mean dressing a wound, splinting a fracture, or keeping a victim calm.

5. *Prevent infection.* This involves cleaning the wound and dressing it to prevent further contamination.

6. *Relieve pain, fear, and anxiety.* Part of first-aid responsibility is to keep an injured victim calm and comfortable.

Specifics of First Aid

CUTS, ABRASIONS, AND BLISTERS

The major danger from cuts is loss of blood. Severity of loss depends on the size and kind of vessels severed. Veins are vessels that return blood from the extremities to the heart. When a vein is severed, the blood flows smoothly from the wound. Bleeding is usually easy to stop.

On the other hand, bleeding from arteries, vessels that carry blood from the heart to the extremities, is rapid and hard to stop. The blood is under high pressure. It spurts from the wound at the same rate as the heartbeat. Spurting blood indicates an emergency. Bleeding must be stopped immediately.

The most reliable and safest way to stop any bleeding is with direct pressure over the wound. If a cut is bleeding badly, don't waste time digging a bandage from your first-aid kit. Apply direct pressure immediately with your bare hand or a clean cloth until you or someone else can find a sterile dressing. Place this over the wound and maintain pressure until bleeding stops.

If possible, raise the injury above heart level to reduce blood pressure to the wound. In most cases, a clot will form within minutes to prevent further bleeding. If bleeding continues, don't remove the original bandage but add new ones over it to soak up blood. A clot should form soon.

If bleeding resumes when you release pressure, a pressure bandage may be needed. Leave in place any sterile pads or cloths you've applied , and wrap a continuous gauze bandage tightly over them. Be careful not to cut off circulation. If the extremity below the wound turns blue, hurts, tingles, or has no pulse, the pressure bandage is too tight. Loosen it slightly to allow better circulation.

A wound severe enough to require a pressure bandage needs professional care. Leave the bandage in place. Don't try to clean the injury. Take the injured person to a doctor.

Most cuts and scrapes aren't that serious. Bleeding is stopped easily. However, this doesn't mean the injury should be ignored. Infection of even a tiny nick or scrape can be serious. The best infection preventive is soap and water. Doctors don't recommend the use of burning treatments such as Merthiolate or iodine, because they destroy tissue. Simply wash the wound with soap and rinse it with running water. Scrub out all gravel, leaves, or other foreign matter. Apply a sterile dressing to prevent further contamination.

If a cut does get infected, it'll swell and turn red and will be extremely tender and painful. Soak the infection several times a day in hot, soapy water, and keep the wound clean. The infection should disappear in 2 or 3 days. If it doesn't, see a doctor.

A clean dressing held with adhesive tape or a gauze bandage is adequate protection for most wounds. A deep laceration should be closed to prevent further injury. Band Aids or butterfly bandages will serve as sutures. To close a scalp laceration, tie strands of hair together over it.

Band-Aids or butterfly bandages can be used to hold a large wound (this one is simulated) closed for proper healing.

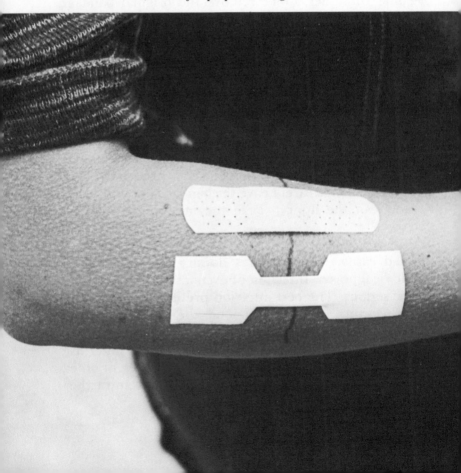

Blisters are probably the most common outdoors injury. They're caused by the rubbing of skin. Blisters may seem insignificant, but they can be incapacitating. One year on a long hike, I got blisters nearly 2 inches across on the balls of both feet. I was unable to continue. Even small blisters can be painful, and the potential for infection exists in any blister.

To prevent blisters, wear one pair of snug socks next to your feet and over these wear a pair of heavier, looser socks so that any rubbing occurs between socks rather than between your feet and socks. During a hike, put on dry socks periodically. If you feel a sore or hot spot developing, check it. If a blister hasn't formed yet, apply moleskin to prevent further rubbing.

If you do get a blister, sterilize a needle or the point of a sharp knife in a flame, poke a hole in the edge of the blister, and squeeze out the fluid. Leave the skin in place for protection. Cover the flattened blister with a bandage to prevent further rubbing. If the blister has already broken, treat it like any open wound. Wash it with soap and water and apply a dressing.

FRACTURES

A fracture is a cracked or broken bone. In the outdoors, fractures most often involve arms and legs.

Fractures are classed two ways: open (compound) and closed (simple). An open fracture is complicated by a skin wound caused by the broken bone itself or by the object that caused the fracture. The important point is that the wound presents danger of contamination and infection. Some authorities say not to wash the wound; others say it should be cleaned and treated the same as any other open wound. The decision probably depends on circumstances. In most cases, you probably should apply a sterile bandage to keep out foreign matter, immobilize the fracture, and get medical help. Don't handle the bone end or try to push it back into place. In a situation where a victim is days from a doctor, severe pain and danger of infection might justify your pulling the bone ends by gentle traction on the limb into a natural position and cleaning the wound.

A closed fracture has no open wound, but some signs leave no doubt that a bone is fractured. The victim may have heard the bone snap. He may be unable to move the injured part, or it may be deformed, crooked, or shorter than the other. With some fractures, the only signs may be intense pain and tenderness, swelling, and bluish or reddish discoloration. In this case, distinguishing a fracture from a sprain or other injury can be hard. Don't manipulate the limb to try to decide. Movement of the broken bone ends can cause severe damage to tissues, nerves, and blood vessels. If suspicious signs are present, assume fracture and treat accordingly. Also, don't try to realign or set a broken bone except to the extent needed to apply a splint. Mild traction, applied by pulling gently on the foot or hand, may be needed to straighten a limb for splinting; but your main objective is simply to immobilize the injury by applying a splint to prevent further damage and to relieve pain.

A first-aid kit on expeditions may include splints, but for average outings, this isn't practicable. As a substitute you might use boards, a walking stick, skis or ski poles, or tree branches. You may even make a splint from a rolled newspaper, a pillow, or heavy clothing that's folded or rolled. Tie the splint into place with rope, nylon webbing, clothing, or cravats.

To prevent rubbing or slipping, pad stiff or abrasive splint materials with clothing or blankets. Tie a splint snugly enough to prevent movement of the fracture but be careful not to pull it so tight that it intensifies pain or reduces circulation. And remember, a splint must extend past joints above and below the break to prevent rotation at these joints. For example, if the forearm is broken, the

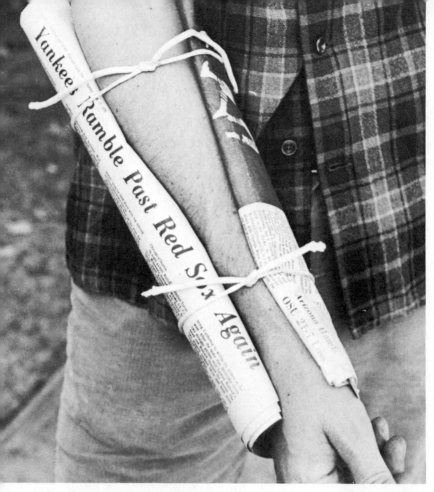

A newspaper used this way serves well as an emergency splint for the lower arm. Splint should extend beyond joint above and below break.

splint should take in the elbow and wrist. For a lower-leg break, the splint should extend beyond the knee and ankle. If the thigh bone is broken, not only should the splint cover the knee and hip, but also the splint on the outside of the leg should extend from the armpit down past the foot. Foot support is important because the lower leg can rotate at the knee, even if the knee is splinted.

For further support of a fractured leg, tie the two legs together. Support a fractured arm in a sling if the elbow is bent. If the elbow is straight, tie the arm to the body.

You can best splint a broken hand or finger by taping the hand around a soft object such as a rolled-up sock. Then support the arm in a sling.

If the collarbone (clavicle) is broken, immobilize it by placing the arm on the injured side in a sling, then tying the sling to the chest to keep the arm from swinging out from the body.

Treat a broken collar bone or broken lower arm by supporting the arm in a sling. Use the large triangular cravat bandage from the survival kit, or improvise a sling, as the author did here with a deer bag.

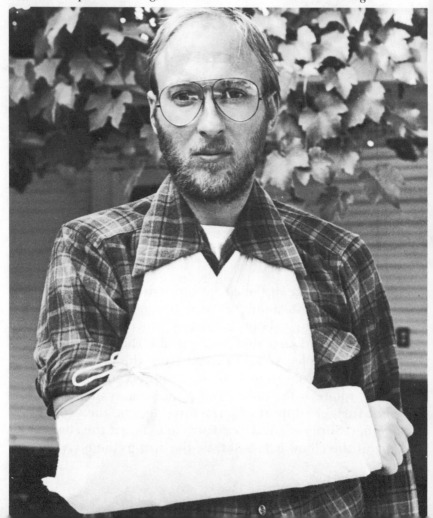

NECK AND BACK INJURIES

Spinal injuries are especially dangerous because even slight movement can damage the spinal cord, causing permanent paralysis.

Signs of spinal injury may be similar to those for other fractures, including pain or tenderness and swelling and redness at the injury site. Occasionally a vertebra will protrude noticeably. Numbness or tingling may accompany a spinal injury. Pain may radiate from the injury to the front of the body or down the arms or legs. The victim may be paralyzed partially.

Under most conditions where medical help or evacuation equipment can be brought to the patient, the best policy is not to move a person with a spinal injury. The victim simply should be made comfortable, kept warm, and maintained in a stationary position. His head should be padded on each side with rolled clothing or blankets to prevent its rotating. If for some reason an injured person must be moved, several people should help, supporting all parts of the body to prevent any twisting or stretching.

A victim of a spinal injury in water can be floated on his back until medical help arrives. Water makes a good support. If the water is cold, threatening hypothermia, a board or other rigid support can be slipped under the injured person to remove him from the water. Again, supporting the sides of his body and head is important to prevent rotation.

DISLOCATIONS

A dislocation is caused by strain on a joint, such as at the shoulder or thumb. Shoulder dislocations are common skiing injuries. They're caused by a fall directly on the shoulder which forces the arm bone out of the shoulder socket.

A dislocated joint looks deformed. It will swell, and pain

will be great, especially during movement. Treat a dislocation as you would a fracture. Unless you've had special training, don't try to replace the dislocated bone. Immobilize it and get medical help.

SPRAINS

Sprains, particularly of the ankle, are common. A sprain is caused by twisting or straining a joint. This abnormal action stretches and tears muscles, ligaments, or tendons.

If the sprain is severe, a splint may help reduce pain by preventing movement. To reduce swelling, a big problem with sprains, keep the injured part elevated and apply cold, wet packs. The injured limb shouldn't be used until initial internal bleeding and swelling subside, in about 24 hours. Then light activity may enhance healing.

BURNS

Open fires, exploding gasoline, scalding liquids, or the sun all can cause burns. Severity of burns depends on three factors: depth, extent, and location.

Depth of burns is defined in degrees. A first-degree burn is the least serious. The skin is red, may be mildly swollen, and is painful. Mild sunburn is a first-degree burn.

Second-degree burns are deeper. Initially the skin is red or mottled, then blisters develop and the area swells.

In third-degree burns, the skin is charred and muscle and organ tissue may be damaged. The burned area may have a white or charred look. Eventually all layers of skin will be lost in that area. All third-degree burns require medical attention because of the serious threat of infection and because skin grafts may be necessary to replace dead skin.

The *extent* of burns is expressed in body area. If more than 15 percent of the body suffers second-degree or third-degree burns, the victim's life is in immediate danger. Roughly, one leg, both arms, the front of the trunk, or the back of the trunk equals 15 percent of the body's surface.

The most serious *location* for a burn is the head or face, because the victim may have inhaled flames, searing the respiratory tract. Any burn in this area requires immediate medical attention.

The objectives of burn treatment are to prevent contamination, to relieve pain, and to treat for shock. First-aid authorities differ on their prescribed treatment. Again, action depends on circumstances. First aid on expeditions requires advanced training and knowledge. Here I'm assuming that medical aid or potential evacuation is no more than a day or two away. Following is a list of first-aid steps for burns:

1. Soak first-degree and second-degree burns in cold water *(not* ice water) until pain subsides.

2. First-degree burns require no further treatment, except protection from abrasion or further burn. Apply sterile dressing for protection.

3. Don't pop blisters or attempt to remove charred skin or clothing from second-degree and third-degree burns.

4. Don't use any kind of ointment, cream, grease, or lotion on second-degree or third-degree burns. These substances increase potential for infection and interfere with cleaning by a doctor.

5. Apply a clean, sterile dressing to second-degree and third-degree burns. If the wound is large, wrap it loosely with roll gauze, then cover this with a bulky, clean bandage or cloth. Leave the dressing in place until a doctor can remove it.

6. A person with second-degree or third-degree burns covering more than 15 percent of his body must get medical attention quickly. Blood serum and other body fluids seep into the wound, greatly reducing blood volume. Severe shock is imminent, and a person can die

within a couple of days unless he receives additional fluids intravenously.

7. If any burn, regardless of its degree or extent, is incapacitating, the victim should get medical aid, particularly for face and neck burns. Inhalation of flames can cause swelling and fluid build-up in the lungs, leading to suffocation.

SUNBURN AND SNOWBLINDNESS

Exposure to sunlight can be healthful, but overexposure can be dangerous, especially at high altitudes where the thin air filters out few of the burning ultraviolet rays. Snow and ice, which reflect ultraviolet rays, greatly magnify the burning effects of sunlight. Most clouds don't block ultraviolet rays, so the effects of sunlight can be as devastating on cloudy days as on sunny ones. Blond- and red-haired people are particularly vulnerable to the effects of the sun.

To prevent sunburn, increase your daily exposure to the sun gradually, in order to develop a tan. Never expose untanned skin to the sun for long periods. Wear protective clothing and wear a hat. Protect exposed skin with a sunscreen ointment or oil that blocks ultraviolet rays. Read the label carefully. Many commercial preparations, often called suntan lotions, are inadequate. In intense sunlight, cover lips, nose, ears, and other sensitive areas with ointment that blocks all sunlight. Most of these contain zinc oxide.

Sunburned skin turns bright red and may blister. The pain can be relieved with cold compresses. Extensive or severe sunburn should be treated as a second-degree burn.

Snowblindness is another danger of intense sunlight. A person may not feel any ill effects during exposure. But then the symptoms may show up several hours later. The eyes will be sensitive and bloodshot and will feel as if they're full of sand. They may be very painful. Snowblindness may disable a person for several days.

Whenever you're on snow or ice, especially at high altitude, wear very dark glasses. Because sunlight reflected off the snow can be as damaging as that coming directly from the sun, the glasses should wrap around or have shields on the sides. Goggles offer good protection. In an emergency, fashion goggles by making narrow slits for the eyeholes in thin cardboard or a piece of cloth, and wear this over the eyes.

If snowblindness occurs, cold compresses on the eyes offer some relief. The eyes should be protected from bright light, and they should not be rubbed. With protection against further exposure, the eyes will heal in a few days.

ARTIFICIAL RESPIRATION

Chest injury, electrocution, near-drowning and carbon-monoxide poisoning can cause respiratory failure. Breathing must be restored quickly to prevent brain damage. Mouth-to-mouth artificial respiration is the best method to restore breathing.

Begin by laying the victim on his back. Check his mouth and throat for obstructions, and clear away anything that might block the airway.

Tilt the victim's head back by lifting gently on the back of the neck and pushing the forehead down. This position (with the lower jaw jutting upward) opens the throat for free air passage. Pinch the victim's nose closed to prevent escape of air, and place your mouth fully on the victim's. On a child, place your mouth over both nose and mouth.

Now blow in. You should see the victim's chest rise. When it does, stop blowing and turn your head to listen for the sound of exhaling air. If the chest doesn't rise when you blow or the air isn't exhaled, check again for obstructions in the mouth and throat. For an adult, repeat the breathing cycle about 12 times a minute—that is, once every 5 seconds. For a child, blow lightly at a rate of 20 times a minute (once every 3 seconds).

A person who was drowning should recover quickly. A person electrocuted or poisoned by carbon monoxide may take a long time to begin breathing on his own, so continue artificial respiration up to an hour.

SHOCK

Shock can follow any injury, and the effects are often more serious than the injury itself. Don't wait for symptoms of shock to appear. Assume they will, and treat for shock following any serious injury.

Shock is the reduction of effective circulating blood to vital organs. The primary cause of shock is reduced blood volume. Bleeding is one cause, but loss of fluids through burns, heavy sweating, vomiting, or diarrhea can also cause shock. Infection and lack of oxygen are other causes of shock. Abnormal changes in body temperature, pain, anxiety, and fear can exaggerate the effects of shock.

A victim in shock is weak and listless. His skin often turns pale, bluish, and clammy. Usually his pulse rate is weak and rapid. He may be nauseated. The symptoms normally occur shortly after injury but may not show up until several hours later. Treat for shock as follows:

1. Lay the victim on his back and raise his legs about a foot above body level to maintain a good blood flow to vital organs. If injuries are on the head or upper body, don't elevate the legs, but raise the victim slightly toward the sitting position.

2. Maintain body warmth. If shock isn't severe, cover the victim with a blanket or sleeping bag. He can maintain his own warmth. In severe cases, blood circulation may be so poor that the victim is unable to produce adequate body heat, so other persons should lie close to warm him

with their heat. Don't warm a shock victim rapidly with sources of heat higher than body temperature.

3. Comfort and reassure the victim. Pain, fear, or the sight of blood can intensify shock. Aspirin or other appropriate pain relief can be given.

4. Keep the victim quiet until all of his injuries have been treated and his pulse is strong and at a normal rate.

If you're alone when seriously injured, expect to get hit with shock. Treat yourself as described immediately while you're still able.

First-Aid Courses

These first-aid suggestions are no substitute for training and practice. A calm head and common sense will help you take care of many problems, but injuries or illness that require specific training may hit you at any time. Everyone should have training in first aid for maximum safety in the field. The American National Red Cross in your area probably offers standard first-aid classes.

Also, make a first-aid kit a permanent part of your outdoors gear. Chapter 15 lists all the items for a first-aid kit.

15
SURVIVAL
EQUIPMENT

Proper equipment plays a big role in outdoors survival, but the best equipment is of no value unless it's available when needed and you know how to use it. Anticipate problems and plan ahead for them by assembling the needed equipment now and by learning how it works.

No equipment list is final. Circumstances vary greatly. Equipment suggestions listed in this chapter are only guidelines drawn from my experience and that of other knowledgeable outdoorsmen. These lists can be altered to meet your specific needs and preferences. The important point is to think ahead: Prepare an adequate equipment kit for your chosen activity, and have it with you whenever you're in the field.

The Survival Pack

To have value, a survival pack must be a constant companion. For that reason, it must be comfortable and convenient. If the pack is cumbersome or heavy, you may decide not to carry it on occasion, and that could be just the time you get caught in a critical situation.

First, what kind of pack is best? Probably most popular is the frameless rucksack. This small, lightweight pack is suitable for most purposes. In some cases, though, a small rucksack with supporting A-frame is better. Such a pack is slightly bulkier than the frameless style, but you can carry more weight comfortably. For instance, you can slip in a heavy wool shirt or down coat, even a sleeping bag, for planned bivouacs.

Personally, I like a belt pack better than a rucksack. It seems more convenient, and I prefer the weight on my hips rather than on my shoulders. A large belt pack holds all the items I consider necessary.

Regardless of pack style, the loaded pack must be light. If it's heavy, you'll dread lugging it around. Choose items carefully, and keep them to a minimum. An adequate survival pack needs to weigh no more than 5 pounds.

Make survival-pack items practically sacred. Put them in the pack, and don't use them under any ordinary circumstances. If an emergency requires you to use a survival-pack item, replace the item as soon as possible. If you delay or forget, you may come up short the next time you need it.

Whenever you head into the field, regardless of the nature or length of your outing, grab that survival pack. Have it with you always. Ideally you'll never need it. But if you do, it could save your life or your companion's.

The following are fundamental survival-pack items:

1. *Flashlight.* Turn one battery backwards (the light won't work that way) so the batteries won't be drained if the switch gets turned on accidentally inside your pack. Carry spare batteries and bulb. Tape these to the flashlight.

2. *Map and Compass.*

3. *Fire-starter material.* Discussed fully in Chapter 8.

4. *Shelter.* I carry a 9' x 12' plastic tarp.

5. *Aluminum cup.* This is essential in order to melt snow or heat water.

6. *Knife.* It should be lightweight but large enough to cut branches or small trees.

7. *Sharpening stone.* A dull knife is worthless. A small stone lets you keep it sharp.

8. *Saw.* This item simplifies cutting poles for emergency shelter. A small folding saw works well, but you may prefer a ring saw or a small hatchet.

9. *First-aid kit.* A complete list of items is found later in this chapter.

10. *Nylon twine or cord.* Carry at least 50 feet for binding poles for emergency shelter, tying splints into place, and many other chores.

11. *Whistle.* Good for distress signalling.

12. *Signal mirror.* If your compass has a mirror, that will do.

13. *Fluorescent plastic flagging.* You can mark a trail for rescuers to follow, or you can mark your backtrail to an emergency campsite.

14. *Small notebook and pencil.* You may have to leave a note for rescuers or write a trip plan to leave at your car or at the trailhead.

15. *Food.* The kinds and quantity will depend largely on conditions. Carry high-energy foods for a couple of extra days.

The following may also be survival-pack items, depending on conditions:

16. *Raingear.* In fall, winter, and spring when precipitation is likely, lightweight raingear should be standard.

17. *Extra socks.* A midday change of socks can prevent blisters.

18. *Sunburn protection.* On open snow or water, a good sunscreen could save a trip.

19. *Snakebite kit.* If venomous snakes inhabit your area, make this a standard item.

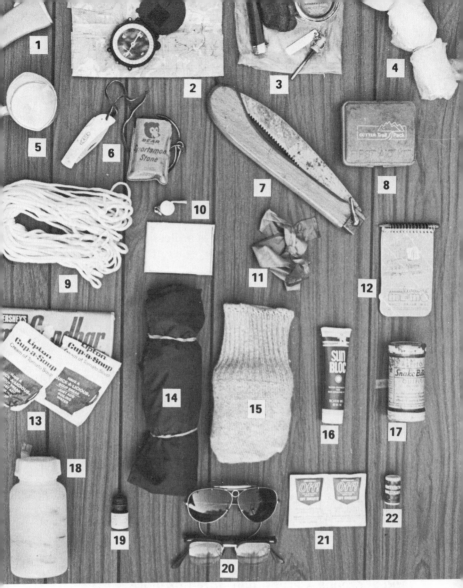

This layout shows the contents of the author's survival kit, which he carries in a large belt pack: 1) flashlight, 2) map and compass, 3) fire-starting materials (in this instance a butane lighter, steel wool, Sterno, and Metal Match), 4) a 9' x 12' plastic tarp, 5) aluminum cup, 6) knife, 7) sharpening stone, 8) folding saw, 9) first-aid kit, 10) 50' of nylon cord, 11) whistle, 12) signal mirror, 13) fluorescent plastic tape, 14) notebook and pencil, 15) emergency food, 16) raingear, 17) extra socks, 18) sunburn preventive, 19) snakebite kit, 20) water bottle, 21) water-purification tablets, 22) sunglasses, 23) spare prescription glasses, 24) insect repellent, 25) salt.

20. *Plastic water bottle.* In snow or desert country, ready water is scarce. Carry water with you.

21. *Water-purification tablets.* In many areas, water is impure. Carry halazone or iodine tablets to make it drinkable.

22. *Dark glasses.* These are eyesavers on snow or water.

23. *Extra eye glasses.* If you can't get along without glasses or contact lenses, have an extra pair on hand.

24. *Insect repellent.* Repellent is a blessing in mosquito or black-fly country.

25. *Salt or salt tablets.* Under extreme conditions, salt depletion could be a problem.

First-Aid Kit

The size and complexity of a first-aid kit will depend on its purpose and how it will be carried. A car kit may be elaborate and fairly heavy, but a kit carried in a survival pack must be compact and light. In assembling first-aid items, consider your possible needs, the number of people in the party, length of stay, and space and weight limitations. The following items might be considered adequate for a backpacking or camping trip of several days:

1. *Band-Aids.* These cover small wounds and can be used to suture lacerations. A versatile item. Carry plenty, a dozen or more.

2. *Sterile 3" x 3" dressings.* These are used on larger cuts and abrasions. Carry a half-dozen or more.

3. *Adhesive tape.* This secures dressings and bandages.

4. *Gauze roll.* This is used for wrapping extensive injuries or making pressure bandages. Good size is 1" x 126".

5. *Aspirin.* Aspirin can relieve minor pain. On longer outings, a stronger pain medicine such as Empirin with codeine may be advisable. This must be obtained by prescription.

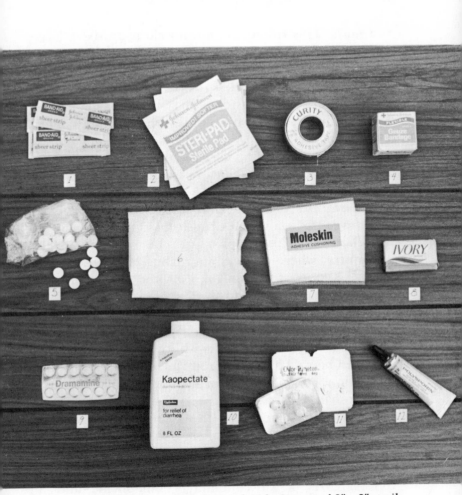

Contents of author's first-aid kit: 1) Band-Aids, 2) several 3" x 3" sterile pads, 3) adhesive tape, 4) gauze roll, 5) aspirin, 6) large triangular cravat bandage, 7) moleskin, 8) soap, 9) Dramamine, 10) medicine for diarrhea, 11) Chlor-Trimeton for hay fever, 12) antibiotic ointment. 13) Not shown—Persons hypersensitive to stings should consult own doctor for a suitable prescription.

6. *Cravat.* This triangular muslin cloth can be a large bandage, a sling for a broken arm or collarbone, a wrapping for a sprained ankle, or a tie for splints.

7. *Moleskin.* This is priceless for covering rubbed skin to prevent blisters. All drugstores carry it.

8. *Small bar of soap.* Wash wounds with soap and water to prevent infection.

In addition to carrying these items, you may want to follow the advice of some doctors and carry medicines for some common maladies:

9. *Nausea and vomiting.* Dramamine, 50 mg., can be bought over the counter at drugstores.

10. *Diarrhea.* This problem can be common in the backcountry, where dishwashing habits may be less than perfect. Kaopectate, available at the drugstore, or Lomotil, prescribed by your doctor, are good.

11. *Hay Fever.* Sudafed, 30 mg., or Chlor-Trimeton, 4 mg., can be bought without prescription.

12. *Infection.* An antibiotic with low incidence of side effects can be valuable. Erythromycin, obtainable through prescription, is good. Polysporin or a similar ointment is good for shallow scratches, broken blisters, and abrasions. No prescription is needed. (Check the ingredients to be sure it contains none you're allergic to.)

13. *Hypersensitivity to stings.* Persons with known hypersensitivity should check with their own doctors and probably carry a kit containing epinephrine and an antihistamine. This must be obtained through a doctor.

Automobile Safety Equipment

The following equipment list might be considered complete for a person taking his rig onto backroads, where the potential for breakdown and getting stuck is great and where help may be miles away. Ordinary highway travelers, however, also can get caught in blizzards or have car trouble on deserted roads. So even on the main highways, drivers should carry safety equipment suited to the conditions they may encounter:

1. *Jack.* A heavy bumper jack such as the Handyman jack is good not only for changing tires but also for jacking a rig out of mud or snow.

2. *Spare tires.* One spare may be adequate, but two give a much wider margin of safety. If you're going into rough, isolated country, a tire-repair kit—including a pump— should be added.

3. *Shovel and ax or saw.* These are essential for digging out of mud or snow or clearing windfalls that may block a road.

4. *Tire chains.* Chains give the best possible traction on mud and snow.

5. *Tow chain.* This heavy-duty chain (or cable) with hooks at each end should be 20 to 30 feet long for assisting stuck or inoperable vehicles.

6. *Tool kit.* You may have little mechanical knowledge, but at the least have an assortment of screwdrivers and wrenches and a pair of pliers to perform simple repairs.

7. *Baling wire.* Wire is always handy for holding a broken tailpipe in place or repairing a broken tire chain.

8. *Jumper cables.* Particularly in cold weather, a battery can be drained of power quickly.

9. *Fan belt.* A broken fan belt can put a rig out of operation.

10. *Flashlight.* One with a powerful, long-lasting beam can be priceless.

11. *Flares and reflectors.* Railroad flares or auto reflectors are used to warn other cars if you're stalled on the highway. For backcountry, carry signal flares.

12. *First-aid kit.* For carrying in a vehicle, this should have an extensive range of items.

13. *Fire starters.* If you're stranded for a long period, you may not want to run the engine constantly for warmth. Then you'll want to get out and light a fire.

Fundamental vehicle safety items: 1) heavy bumper jack, 2) spare tire
(and lug wrench); two spares give wider safety margin, 3) ax or saw,
and shovel, 4) tire chains, 5) tow chain, 6) tool kit, 7) baling wire, 8)
jumper cables, 9) fan belt, 10) flashlight, 11) signal flares, 12) first-aid
kit, 13) fire-starting materials, 14) emergency rations, 15) maps and
compass, 16) fire extinguisher, 17) five gallons of water, 18) desert still,
19) bag of sand or gravel, 20) windshield scraper, 21) blankets or
sleeping bags.

14. *Emergency rations.* Extra food can be welcome if you're caught or stranded for some time. Freeze-dried foods are easy to stow, and they keep forever. Carry enough for 3 days or more.

15. *Maps and compass.*

16. *Fire extinguisher.* Wherever gasoline is used, fire is a threat.

17. *Five gallons of water.* This should be for both drinking and for use in a vehicle's cooling system. Carrying extra water is particularly important in the desert.

Additional items should also be carried, depending on the season:

18. *Desert still.* During hot weather, have a large piece of clear plastic, a piece of rubber tubing, and a can to make a survival still (see page 44).

19. *Bag of sand or gravel.* In winter, traction on ice may be a problem. Sand or gravel spread in front of the tires can give needed traction.

20. *Ice scraper.* A clear view through the windshield is essential for safe driving.

21. *Blankets or sleeping bags.* If you're stranded in bitter weather, the major problem could be staying warm. In fall, winter and spring, when the potential for winter storms exists, always carry these items to insure warmth.

Snowmobile Safety Equipment

When you use mechanical equipment, it's impossible to carry spare parts and tools to handle every potential problem. But you should have equipment to deal with common problems. Don Stonehill recommends the following items:

1. *Spare drive belt.* A snowmobile drive belt undergoes constant wear, so breakage isn't uncommon. When the belt goes, the machine stops. Carry a spare under the seat, and know how to put it on.

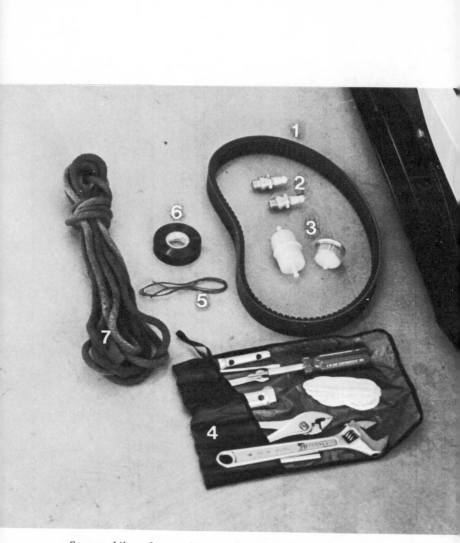

Snowmobile safety equipment should include: 1) spare drive belt, 2) extra spark plugs (wrench for them in tool kit), 3) spare fuel filter (two kinds shown here), 4) tool kit, 5) baling wire, 6) plastic tape, 7) tow rope.

2. *Extra spark plugs and plug wrench.* Fouled plugs are predictable. Plugs may have to be replaced in the field.

3. *Fuel filter.* Particles in low-grade fuel or dirt in the tank can clog a fuel filter.

4. *General-purpose wrench and other basic tools.* A snowmobile vibrates excessively, so loose nuts and bolts are a common problem. Most machines have three or four standard sizes of nuts and bolts. Carry a wrench or wrenches to fit these, plus a screwdriver and pliers.

5. *Baling wire.* This might be used to repair a loose muffler, broken brake handle or ski, or other damaged parts.

6. *A roll of black plastic tape.* This can be used for wrapping wires and repairing minor breaks.

7. *Tow rope—20 feet long.* This is essential in case of a major breakdown. One machine can pull another to safety.

In addition, a snowmobiler should have general emergency equipment such as flashlight, first-aid kit, spare rations, and other items. A survival pack, as described earlier in this chapter, can be carried to insure that these items are always on hand.

Boating Safety Equipment

Much equipment listed here is legally required in most areas for motorboats. The kind of equipment you carry will depend on circumstances such as the size of the boat and the kind of water you're on. This list might be considered standard for inland outboard boating:

1. *Life preservers,* also known as personal floatation devices (PFDs). These should be Coast Guard-approved, and every person in the boat should have one.

2. *Oars or paddles.* You often can row or paddle to safety in case of engine breakdown.

For outboard boating, these safety items might be considered standard: 1) life preserver (one Coast Guard-approved model for each passenger), 2) at least one paddle, or pair of oars, 3) bailing bucket, 4) fire extinguisher, 5) compass and maps or charts, 6) 50' of rope, 7) distress signals, 8) running lights, 9) spare parts, 10) tools.

3. *Bailing device.* Under rough conditions, you could take on water. Have a bucket or can to bail with.

4. *Fire extinguisher.* Anywhere gasoline is used, fire is a danger. Water won't put out a petroleum fire.

5. *Compass and maps or charts.*

6. *Fifty feet or more of rope or line.* This can be used for towing a disabled boat, tying up to shore, or rigging a sea anchor.

7. *Distress signals.* Signal flares can be seen for miles over water. A mirror is also good. For audible signalling, carry a whistle or small horn powered by a pressurized can.

8. *Running lights.* These are legally required on most boats. Check state regulations.

9. *Spare parts.* For outboards, these should include at least an extra propeller, shear pins, cotter pins, and spark plugs.

10. *Tools.* A minimum kit should contain pliers, crescent wrench, screwdriver, and spark-plug wrench.

Here again, the survival pack mentioned earlier in this chapter can be included to provide flashlight, first-aid kit, and other general emergency items.

INDEX

Index